Wounded Heroes

Wounded Heroes

The Secrets of
Charles Spurgeon, Hudson Taylor,
Amy Carmichael, C.S. Lewis, Isobel Kuhn,
Ruth Bell Graham, and others who
triumphed over pain

Elizabeth R. Skoglund

Illustrations by John Whorrall

A Raven's Ridge Book

BAKER BOOK HOUSE
Grand Rapids, Michigan 49516

Wounded Heroes

To Ken and Carolyn Connolly

CONTENTS

VIGNETTES

ACKNOWLEDGMENTS

Researching the material for *Wounded Heroes* was a herculean task. Then condensing and connecting the material into something which would not only help the reader but would whet his or her appetite for reading more of the writings of these great saints presented an even greater challenge. Many people helped in this task, for in the writing of any book, one does not do it alone.

Once again I am indebted to Stephen Griffith who so often makes things happen. His appreciation of the value of past writings is an ongoing encouragement, along with the ever-present support of my agent Richard Baltzell.

Ken and Carolyn Connolly and John and Lynn Whorrall helped fill in research details and, along with University Bible Church and a substantial group of otherwise unrelated people who committed to regular prayer, offered consistent prayer support as well.

Various individuals at Overseas Missionary Fellowship (Formerly China Inland Mission) were helpful in sending books, looking up and duplicating material, and locating people who could give further information. Eileen Kuhn and Henry and Mary Guinness (Geraldine Taylor's nephew) were kind in their willingness to grant interviews. Evelyn Freeland was once again helpful in gathering material and in coordinating time with Ruth Bell Graham, who, along with her eldest daughter Gigi Graham Tchividjian, gave generously of her time.

My usual debt of gratitude goes to Rayne Wagner for her detailed work on footnotes and permissions and to Marilyn Pendleton for practical details too numerous to mention. Of equal value has been their enthusiasm for the importance of this volume.

In the writing of this book there were times when I related to Churchill's words which were uttered at the time he accepted the Nobel Prize for Literature for his six volumes of the Second World War. He said: "Writing a book is an adventure. To begin with it is a toy, an amusement; and then it becomes a master, and then it becomes a tyrant. And the last phase is that, just as you are about to be reconciled to your servitude, you kill the monster."

Yet for all the hard work, the joy of doing this book was still greater. Someone once said that "The worth of a thing well done is to have done it." Out of the more than twenty books which I have written, no book has been as uplifting to me personally. Writing of the lives and works of these people has been like going to a spiritual retreat. I have been refreshed, lifted up, and challenged. I have been amazed at the timelessness of biblical truth. Just to have done the job ultimately became a reward in itself.

NO SCAR?

Hast thou no scar?
No hidden scar on foot, or side, or hand?
I hear thee sung as mighty in the land,
I hear them hail thy bright ascendant star,
Hast thou no scar?

Hast thou no wound?
Yet I was wounded by the archers, spent,
Leaned Me against a tree to die; and rent
By ravening beasts that compassed Me, I swooned:
Hast thou no wound?

No wound? no scar?
Yet, as the Master shall the servant be,
And pierced are the feet that follow Me;
But thine are whole: can he have followed far
Who has nor wound nor scar?[1]

—Amy Carmichael

CHAPTER 1

Living in a Tension-Filled World

A few years back, as I lay in a hammock overlooking the deep blue waters of the Zihuatanejo Bay, Mexico, I felt I could handle anything. The hot tropical sun was at its afternoon peak but I was shielded from it by a large tree with enormous leaves. Looking out over the water was an experience of sheer tranquillity. Up and down the beach I could see singular figures at various places, napping, reading or just resting under shelter from the sun.

My body relaxed in the afternoon heat. No deadlines pressed on on me. No telephone was available if someone had wanted to reach me. No appointments were written into my purse-size date book. It was the closest I had come in a long time to eradication of all pain. No pressure. No worry. No irritation. Yet when I remembered that in the morning I would have to get up early to catch a plane to Mexico City and then home, I knew with a twinge of sadness that I had not eradicated pain. All the pressures of ordinary life would undoubtedly be waiting when I arrived home. But I had refurbished my strength and developed a greater ability to go on.

According to some Christians if a person is really walking with God, suffering and pain are eradicated and life is lived in freedom from stress. To such, prayer which does not receive a "Yes" answer is called "unanswered prayer." "Unanswered prayer" usually means that the petitioner is somehow to blame. The notion that God could say "Wait" or even "No" is inconceivable to those with this mentality.

Realistically, however, pain, stress, tension, grief: these are never eradicated from this earthly life of ours. Occasionally a vacation or even a special day-outing can provide temporary respite. My times in Mexico and my weekends by the ocean are good examples of this. Sometimes, too, we may experience miraculous answers to prayer. A cancer is healed; a job is salvaged; the prodigal child returns. But ultimately suffering remains part of the condition of mankind. And in the end we all experience physical death.

Stress and Pressure, a Daily Occurrence

Day by day we each are confronted by the stress and pressure of everyday life, at both monumental and small levels. We file our tax return and discover we owe more. We plan an outing and it rains. We finish a report late at night and our printer breaks down.

Then there are always the "what ifs." The next pap smear or mammogram may indicate cancer. The next person eliminated from our place of work may be ourselves. The newest accident statistic could be our loved one. Life at its best is uncertain. Drive-by shootings and terrorist attacks; earthquakes, hurricanes, and floods; financial crunches and problems in health care: all these, added to the individualized tensions and suffering which are private to each human being, illustrate beyond a doubt that pain is indeed an absolute in every life.

Sometimes the solutions are not all spiritual. A malfunctioning thyroid gland may create a state of depression, or childhood abuse can produce a series of events which result in a fearful adult or an abusive parent. Furthermore, the intertwining of body, mind, and spirit are frequently impossible to separate from each other. For that reason, among others, the best solution for most of us as we deal with life's problems lies in the resources which are to be found in the combination of physical health, emotional wholeness, and, above all, the Indwelling Christ.

The basic message of the wounded heroes of this book is that we can find meaning in the middle of suffering; we can cope with the multitude of trivial irritations which bombard each of our lives; and we can do more than just survive.

Such a viewpoint is not meant to imply that pain is wonderful or that it should be cultivated just because that pain can contribute to growth. To the contrary, any normal person will go to great lengths to avoid pain. What we are talking about here is unavoidable pain, suffering which does not immediately go away, even when we try to get rid of it.

In contrast to many of our misconceptions regarding our tendency to focus on happiness and the eradication of pain, Dr. Joseph Fabry of the

Institute of Logotherapy states his views simply and concisely in the context of Logotherapy, a therapy of meaning. Says Fabry:

> "What I gained from Logotherapy is the recognition that central to man's life is the pursuit of meaning, and not the pursuit of happiness; that we only invite frustration if we expect life to be primarily pleasurable; that life imposes obligations, and that pleasure and happiness come from responding to the tasks of life."

In this statement by Dr. Fabry, and indeed in the writings of Dr. Viktor Frankl who developed the ideas of Logotherapy, several concepts are clear. Effective living involves a focus on dealing with problems in a way which ultimately means transcending them and going beyond them, at least for a time, not eradicating them. We have certainly not been promised a rose garden; but then we have not been set down in the midst of thorns either. When we are realistic, we see life as having both pain and pleasure.

When we view life from this vantage point we will cease to berate ourselves for being so unspiritual as to suffer. Instead, we will accept God's gift of inner joy and find happiness in living lives content in a task. Meaning will be found, not lost, in suffering. For although we try by all means to avoid pain, there are times when it cannot be eradicated. Then the best solution to handling that suffering is to find some meaning in it.

Only Children Believe That Pain Always Goes Away

In real life only children believe that pain always goes away; and even they learn quickly that such is not the case. Only the insane achieve in actuality the eradication of all pain; and they do it by denying reality, not by finding it.

In this century and in this country we look upon happiness and freedom from pain as inalienable rights, the reward for a person who manages his life well. Our worship of pleasure feeds this. So does our distorted view of the "normal Christian life." We easily become disillusioned with our lives. We forget what Christ told us—that in this life we would have sorrow. We quote verses referring to the joy of God without defining the word "joy." We forget the ups and downs, the delights and despair of the psalmist David. And we often forget that even in all of David's distress of mind and anguish of soul, he was the one described in Scriptures as a man after God's own heart.

In contrast to the current barrage of literature which promises fast answers, instant success, and unending happiness to those who read and follow these, earlier figures in Christian thinking promised no such things. But what they did offer was realistic and it worked.

As we shall see, these saints were flesh and blood human beings with real problems. They were at times wounded in their respective journeys through life. But because of the way they dealt with pain, by definition they became heroes.

Eradication of pain in this life is an unrealistic expectation. We deceive ourselves and others if we deny this. Several years ago I was on a talk show with another guest who directed a Christian organization. At the outset this man turned to the talk show host and said: "I have never felt anger since the day I became a Christian."

The host turned to me and laughed, "Then we're in for an interesting show since you just wrote a book on anger!"

The show went on, and several questions were directed to me about my book. The idea of our conflict on the subject did not come up until the end of the two-hour show when my friend said vehemently: "You know, I get so angry at Satan!"

There was dead silence and then a roar of laughter from the talk show host. Even my friend here had not eradicated anger. He just hoped he had, and had tried to make himself believe that he had succeeded. He viewed eradication, not coping, as the solution to life's problems.

As children, and even as adults, we try hard to eradicate unpleasant emotions from our lives. Sometimes we try so fervently that we even believe we have succeeded, until we are jolted back into reality by the obvious recurrence of those feelings. But in actuality, all feelings—pleasant as well as unpleasant—are part of life. The great challenge is to use unavoidable pain for growth. Then it is in the contrast between pain and pleasure that true happiness is really felt; and it is in their tension and conflict that we often grow.

In a sense, the tranquillity of the Zihuatanejo Bay would have been flat and lifeless had it not been experienced in contrast to the tension of life. The relaxation alone would not have reenergized me. It would have lulled me into a deadly depression, leading to emptiness, not to a task.

D. Martyn Lloyd-Jones

Martyn Lloyd-Jones was a Harley Street physician who became a preacher and the handpicked successor of G. Campbell Morgan in England.

"'Christianity is Christ.' It is not a philosophy, indeed not even a religion. It is the good news that 'God hath visited and redeemed his people' and that He has done so by sending His only begotten Son into this world to live, and die, and rise again. Our Lord Jesus Christ is 'the Alpha and Omega, the First and the Last'. In other words, He is the one Authority."[1]

"What many are tending to do today is this. They say, 'Take up Christianity. It will pay you. I am a witness to it.' So a short address is given, and people are then called upon to testify. Why are people expected to want to accept Christianity? Because it works. It does this or that. It promises you happiness. It gives you peace and joy. I suggest that this is false evangelism. Our one business is to preach the Lord Jesus Christ, the final Authority. We are

(1899–1981)

told to declare Him, and that men and women are to come face to face with Him. The cults can give you 'results'. Christian Science can tell you that if you do this and that you will sleep well at night, you will stop worrying, you will feel healthier, and you will lose your aches and pains. All the cults can do that sort of thing. We are not to do that. We are to declare Him, and to bring people face to face with Him. That was His own method.

"The whole of the New Testament is clearly designed to convince us of the authority of Jesus Christ. It is clear that if He is not who He claims to be, there is no need to listen to Him. If He is, then we are bound to listen to Him and to do whatever He may tell us to do. My own happiness is not the criterion. If He allows me to go on being ill or in trouble—whatever He says, I will answer, 'Yes, Lord.' I will do so because He is the Lord. He is the Authority."[2]

CHAPTER 2

Divine Spending Money

"No place is so deep, that he is not deeper still." This concept which forms the underlining message of the movie "The Hiding Place" is what comes to my mind when I think of Corrie Ten Boom, the dutch watchmaker's daughter who helped save Jews in Holland during the Holocaust. The words are reminiscent, too, of nineteenth Century preacher F.B. Meyer when he said: "He never puts His sheep forth without going before them...No ascent so steep that we cannot see His form in advance; no stones so sharp that are not flecked with His blood; no fire so intense that One does not go beside us, whose form is like the Son of God; no waters so deep that Emmanuel does not go beside us."[1]

In reading the works of great men and women of God I have been struck by their sense of balance. In the writings of Corrie Ten Boom, and certainly in the movie "The Hiding Place," there is a consistent emphasis on the sufficiency of Christ. He is there in the rat infested cell of the concentration camp, the beatings, the dying. He is her sufficiency in circumstances which go beyond human endurance. He is there when the suffering remains, when the pain does not go away.

Yet, in later years, when Miss Ten Boom was writing and speaking of that All Sufficient One, a person who worked closely with her, said to me: "Corrie Ten Boom had less self hate than anyone I knew." He continued: "She believed that God had a work for her to do and she did it. She didn't go around questioning whether she was doing it right or not." In missionary Amy Carmichael's terms, she didn't look back upon past guidance. She trusted her Lord to guide, and she had confidence in her perception of that

21

leading. She combined a deep spiritual reality with a healthy sense of positive self worth.

Similarly F.B. Meyer's biographer W.G. Fullerton said of Meyer: "His transparency and simplicity were his charm: he was humble, but not falsely modest: with a just estimate of his own powers he spoke again and again of some new enterprise as 'The greatest work of my life,' taking the greatness of it all for granted."[2]

Yet the self confidence which Corrie Ten Boom and F.B. Meyer embraced should not be misunderstood for the me-ism of our time, which is truly more indicative of insecurity and self-doubt than it is of a God-given self confidence. For in Meyer's words: "Selfishness, of every kind, in its activities, or its introspection, is a hurtful thing, and shuts out the help and love of God....The soul, occupied with its own griefs, and refusing to be comforted, becomes presently a Dead Sea, full of brine and salt, over which birds do not fly, and besides which no green thing grows. And thus we miss the very lesson God would teach us. His constant war is against the self-life, and every pain He inflicts is to lesson its hold on us...."[3]

For those who would say "Why Me?" to pain, and insist that it is part of good self confidence to demand an instant granting of their own desires from God, as if he were a cosmic Santa Claus or a Giant Tranquilizer, Meyer offers the example of a Hindu woman, who according to legend lost her only child. "Wild with grief, she implored a prophet to give back her little one to her love. He looked at her for a long while tenderly, and said, 'Go, my daughter, bring me a handful of rice from a house into which Death has never entered, and I will do as thou desirest.' The woman at once began her search. She went from dwelling to dwelling, and had no difficulty in obtaining what the prophet specified; but when they had granted it, she inquired, 'Are you all here around the hearth—father, mother, children—none missing?' But the people invariably shook their heads with sighs and looks of sadness; for far and wide as she wandered, there was always some vacant seat by the hearth. And gradually, as she passed on, the narrator says, the waves of her grief subsided before the spectacle of sorrow everywhere, and her heart, ceasing to be occupied with its own selfish pang, flowing out in strong yearnings of sympathy with the universal suffering, tears of anguish softened into tears of pity, passion melted away in compassion; she forgot herself in the general interest, and found redemption in redeeming."[4]

A woman I saw in counseling after the death of her husband, told me of the months of illness which the man had endured prior to his death.

Just about the time I thought she was going to ask "Why me?" she said: "You know, those months were happy ones. I loved him so much. I miss him, but death is part of life. I can't expect to avoid it."

The woman did not profess a faith in Christ. But I couldn't help but contrast her to a young man whom I had seen a few weeks later who, after describing the loss of a girl friend, almost screamed at me the words: "I hate her for hurting me and God's not going to stop me from resenting Him for doing this to me. I trusted Him, and look what He did?" This young man had decided that he only wanted God as long as God did what pleased him. He had put himself as the God of his life and the result was added pain.

A person who truly possess a good self image will have, as a result of that confidence, a greater capacity to understand and accept the limitations of human wisdom as well as the desirability and, indeed, the obligation to trust God in the dark when that becomes necessary. If they choose to live in the power of that potential, such a person will not ask "Why me?"; instead he or she may ask "Why not me?"

God never advocates self hate. But He does teach a hatred for sin and the sin nature of Romans six and a consequent turning from selfishness. Moreover, God doesn't set us free from the bondage of self hate to allow us to be enslaved by the bondage of self worship. Not long ago I went into a coffee house book store which was located in a shopping area just off of the ocean. I was on vacation, and had come to browse. I picked up a book where the author had dedicated the book to herself. I practically bumped into a large cut-out cardboard picture of Katharine Hepburn standing over a stack of her books entitled *Me*. A large number of the best seller books, as well as the psychology and self help books, focused on self worship. Topping it all, was a quote from the Gnostic Gospels: "If you bring forth what is within you, what you bring forth will save you. If you do not bring forth what is within you, what you do not bring forth will destroy you." According to the footnote this was written by a man named Jesus, who did *not* claim to be the Son of God and who wrote two centuries after the death of our Lord Jesus Christ.[5]

The concept of self worship is not a new one, nor is its direct espousal peculiar to our day. At the time most of the heroes of this book were preaching and writing, nineteenth century poet Walt Whitman wrote, "I celebrate myself, and sing myself"; and Ralph Waldo Emerson was talking about the spark of the divine within each man and woman. Yet there is not the most remote similarity between Emerson's spark of the divine or today's me-ism and the biblical truth of "Christ in Me." Nor is good self esteem related to self worship.

True recovery and good self esteem are quite different from groveling in either self hate or blatant self promotion. Medieval scholar C.S. Lewis sees the focus as God in us rather than a glorification of man, himself, without God. In *Mere Christianity* Lewis warns: "Make no mistake," He says, "if you let me, I will make you perfect. The moment you put yourself in My hands, that is what you are in for. Nothing less, or other, than that. You have free will, and if you choose, you can push Me away. But if you do not push Me away, understand that I am going to see this job through. Whatever suffering it may cost you in your earthly life, whatever inconceivable purification it may cost you after death, whatever it costs Me, I will never rest, nor let you rest, until you are literally perfect—until my Father can say without reservation that he is well pleased with you, as He said He was well pleased with me. This I can do and will do. But I will not do anything less."[6]

F.B. Meyer puts it somewhat differently: "The first step towards self reverence is to see God, to worship Him, to bow down before Him, to know that He is God alone, and then we begin to reverence the nature made in His image, which we are to hold sacred for His sake."[7]

In a way which is constant with the sermons of that giant of nineteenth century preachers, Charles H. Spurgeon, Meyer, too, is acutely aware of the frailty of the human body and how it relates to the wholeness, or lack of wholeness, of the mind. A tired body can create the depths of depression and self hate. Says Meyer: "The sense of failure often arises from an overtaxed nervous system, which has been strung almost to breaking-point, and has suddenly collapsed. It was so with Elijah, when he lay beneath the juniper tree, and asked for death. But He who knows our frame knew better than to send the Angel of Death, and commissioned another to provide him with food and sleep. Often, after some great deliverance, the late Dr. Maclaren would be overwhelmed with the sense of failure. 'I must not speak again on such an occasion,' would be his exclamation, whilst the whole audience, as they dispersed, went away inspired and blessed. We must always allow for the depression which comes from the rebound of the overstrung bow."[8]

Furthermore Meyer, like C.S. Lewis, gives credence to the fine but concrete difference between psychological problems and sin. People who have emotional problems are not necessarily sinning. "We do not blame the maniac who seeks to fire a cathedral: we simply confine him; his will was impaired. But we condemn the man who clearly meant to take his brother's life, though the deed itself was frustrated; his will was murder."[9]

The basis for the free functioning of "Christ in Me" is the Lordship of Christ. The English poet Tennyson put it concisely: "Our wills are ours to make them Thine." Hymn writer George Matheson wrote with words which are as contemporary for our time as they were for his:

> Make me a captive, Lord,
>   And then I shall be free;
> Force me to render up my sword,
>   And I shall conq'ror be.
> I sink in life's alarms
>   When by myself I stand;
> Imprison me within Thine arms,
>   And strong shall be my hand.
>
> My heart is weak and poor
>   Until it master find:
> It has no spring of action sure,
>   It varies with the wind:
> It cannot freely move
>   Till Thou has wrought its chain.
> Enslave it with Thy matchless love,
>   And deathless it shall reign.
>
> My power is faint and low
>   Till I have learned to serve:
> It wants the needed fire to glow,
>   It wants the breeze to nerve;
> It cannot drive the world
>   Until itself be driven;
> Its flag can only be unfurled
>   When Thou shalt breathe from heaven.
>
> My will is not my own
>   Till Thou has made it Thine;
> If it would reach the monarch's throne
>   It must its crown resign:
> It only stands unbent
>   Amid the clashing strife,
> When on Thy bosom it has leant,
>   And found in Thee its life.[10]

It is the nature of life on this earth to be in bondage to someone or something. As a counselor I see people who are enslaved to other people or to a chemical or to their own passions. I also see those who choose to be the bondslave of Jesus Christ. The paradox is that only in such a choice is real freedom found.

Meyer uses the image of a house:

> "He stands at the door and knocks; if any will open the door He will come in. Are you willing to let Him in? Are you willing for Him to do what He likes with you and yours?—If so, He will begin to fulfill in you the good pleasure of His goodness and the work of faith with power; and you may write on the lentel of your life, 'This house has passed into other hands, and will be opened under entirely new management.'"[11]

> Yet sometimes "Instead of occupying all, our gracious Guest has been confined to one or two back rooms of our hearts; as a poor housekeeper is sometimes put in to keep a mansion, dwelling in attic or cellar; while the suites of splendid apartments are consigned to dust—sheets and cobwebs, shuttered, dismantled, and locked."[12]

> Concludes Meyer: "You never will be happy until you let the Lord Jesus keep the house of your nature, closely scrutinizing every visitor and admitting only His friends. He must reign. He must have all or none. He must have the key of every closet, of every cupboard, and of every room. Do not try to make them fit for Him. Simply give Him the key. He will cleanse and renovate and make beautiful."[13]

Giving oneself up to the Lordship of Christ doesn't mean that self hate is the only appropriate prerequisite. To the contrary, such an act of committal has greater meaning when one surrenders to God something which has personal value. For to give away that which you hate does not involve sacrifice. It is simply an act of rational behavior resulting from desperation.

Similarly, understanding the fundamental truth of "Christ in Me" as the true source of wholeness, does not mean that psychological help can not be used by God as a means of putting theology into shoeleather, of helping a person take biblical principles and make them part of practical everyday living.

A young man who lost his job through no fault of his own began to drink heavily. Then his wife left him and he found himself drinking even more. One morning he woke up in a street gutter, covered with his own vomit, cry-

Andrew Murray

Andrew Murray was a Scottish preacher who spent many years in South Africa. He was known as a noted conference speaker and devotional writer.

"...Amy Carmichael in *Though the Mountains Shake* tells of an experience in 1895 when Andrew Murray of South Africa was in England taking part in various conventions, and because of a physical breakdown in Japan she had returned home. At one time they were both guests in the same house. 'I knew that his books were very good,' she said. 'Not that I had read one of them, but a neat row of them, dressed in sober grey, lived in my mother's room, and she and everybody said how good they were.' Amy Carmichael wondered if he was as good as his books, and found that he was even better. 'For,' said she, 'there was not only goodness, there was a delicious dry humour, dauntless courage, and the gentleness and simplicity of a dear child. And he was very loving. He never seemed to be tired of loving.'

(1829–1917)

"Then something painful happened to Mr. Murray. Miss Carmichael records that this is how he met it:

> "'He was quiet for a while with his Lord, then he wrote these words for himself:
>
> First, he brought me here, it is by His will I am in this strait place: in that fact I will rest. Next, he will keep me here in His love, and give me grace to behave as His child. Then, He will make the trial a blessing, teaching me the lessons He intends me to learn, and working in me the grace He means to bestow. Last, in His good time He can bring me out again—how and when He knows. Let me say I am here,
>
> (1) By God's appointment,
> (2) In His keeping,
> (3) Under His training,
> (4) For His time.'"[1]

CHAPTER 3

Wounded Heroes

It was a sunny afternoon many years ago. I was fifteen. School was out for the day, and I had a long wait before the carpool which I was in left for home. But I had a new book, Hudson Taylor's Spiritual Secret, to help me pass the afternoon. I settled down comfortably on the grassy slopes which surrounded the school grounds and became lost in the story of Hudson Taylor and the China Inland Mission. The afternoon slipped away, but I was never again the same. Two truths stood out in my mind which were to remain there for the rest of my life: Christ in me, the key to Christian living, and God's work done in God's way will receive God's supply.

Founder of the China Inland Mission, Hudson Taylor, knew that God does not eliminate need. But instead of employing cheap methods in order to support his work, he discovered a great principle of the Christian life: God's work, done in God's way, will receive God's supply. This principle worked, not only for Hudson Taylor in China, but for George Muller and his orphanages in England, and for Amy Carmichael in her work rescuing children dedicated to the gods in South India.

From as far back as I could remember, I had heard of Hudson Taylor. At the time of my birth my Aunt Ruth was in China as a missionary under that great mission. I had been read to from childhood story books about Hudson Taylor, his extraordinary faith, and his remarkable missionary work in China. I had been shown pictures of my own aunt, wearing her long chinese gown, riding on the backs of mules, and, always, teaching children.

Yet on this particular afternoon as I read of the challenge of Hudson Taylor and the call to total dependence upon God to supply his work, I knew

35

that now Hudson Taylor had influenced my life in a new and permanent way. The old knowledge had been made new for me.

And so it has been with each of those who are highlighted in this book. While, once again it seems to me that, none of them ever were new to me, I can remember with clarity the times when each of them first became significant to me, for me.

Again at the age of fifteen, which was a pivotal year for me spiritually, I was introduced more specifically to the books of Amy Carmichael by one of my teachers. Amy Wilson Carmichael, founder of the Dohnavur Fellowship in India, wrote eloquently on a number of subjects, but with particular insight on the problem of suffering. She viewed life with firm realism: suffering cannot be eliminated from life. Yet in no way did Amy Carmichael feel that God allows us to be tossed around by the whim of fate as we try hopelessly to escape suffering. Neither did she propose that we lie down helplessly under its power. To the contrary, she presented practical help and realistic suggestions that can build hope and meaning into suffering.

The first book which I read by this author was Mimosa. But my first memory is of Star, Mimosa's sister, the little girl in India who sought out the God who could change dispositions. That seemed good enough proof of his power to me too. But more than that, the intellectual basis for my faith in God was strengthened by the idea that a child in the middle of India, who had no knowledge of God, could yet be sought out by Him and found.

Later in college I was impressed also by the similarity between the experience of Star and the words of the English poet, Francis Thompson, in the "Hound of Heaven" where he talks of God's pursuit of man and says: "I am he whom thou seekest!"[1] The same idea is repeated as well in John Donne's famous sonnet, which has remained a favorite of mine, which starts, "Batter my heart, three-personed God. . ."[2] Again, God finding man. Most of all, even at the age of fifteen, the idea which Amy Carmichael presents so well, that nothing matters but that which was eternal, became a safety zone to me for the rest of my life. It became an anchor.

My first year of college was a year of spiritual searching and rebellion for me. Agnosticism held a pseudo-intellectual appeal. It was easy for me to see the idiocy of atheism. After all, how could anyone look around at just creation itself and absolutely deny the existence of a God? But agnosticism, with its brash, "How can man really know beyond that which he can prove in a test tube?" so to speak, held an appeal. "Perhaps," I argued, "I just believe the way I do because it's been taught to me all of my life." Yet way down deep inside I knew, too, that I was rebelling against the basic authority of God in my life. And I realized that I knew too much about God to feel that I could follow Him without total commitment to that authority.

During that year I read a good many books which argued against God. But one book which was life-transforming for me was Mere Christianity by C.S. Lewis. Later in my life Lewis became a major influence in my thinking about subjects like pain and the difference between sin and humanness, a subject not easily understood by many Protestants.

More contemporary, yet certainly untainted by the froth of superficial religious thoughts, C.S. Lewis had enough strength to face and declare that humanness cannot be eradicated and that it is indeed not sinful. Some things are not black and white. There are indeed varying shades of gray. Humanness is one of these. Humanness can be lived with, and even improved upon, but not eradicated. While sin can never be excused in the name of humanness, humanness itself is not sin and should not be treated as such. An understanding of this concept as seen in the writings of C.S. Lewis will keep us truly holy while at the same time we do not become legalistic and harsh.

As I moved toward my last year in college, I had effectively burned out. I remember taking a graduate class in American literature, after receiving permission to do so before I was a graduate. I knew the professor well because I had been his assistant. When the mid-term exam came along, I knew the material well, but I was too ill to think logically. When I went up to his desk to ask the meaning of one of the questions, He looked at me oddly as he answered what was obvious. When I went home I realized I had taken the test with a high fever! A few days later, when I got my paper back, "B-" was written on it with the words, "Betty, this isn't bad for the shape you were in!"

More than two years of a full course at the university, along with almost a full course at a theological seminary combined with teaching sunday school, dating several nights a week, part-time jobs, attending Bible studies, and active participation in Inter-Varsity Christian Fellowship took its toll. After graduating in three and a half years instead of four, with many extra units to spare, I slumped into full-time teaching and wondered why I was so tired.

Much later I learned that these problems had been physically based, first from just over-doing and then from actual physical problems. But for the time I was frightened and confused; and my first instinct was to treat the exhaustion with spiritual methods. I practically memorized Romans six, and ineffectively reckoned myself dead to exhaustion and the results of that exhaustion. It didn't work, for obvious reasons; but instead of seeing that exhaustion didn't fit into the province of sin, I just felt that I had to be missing some great spiritual truth. I couldn't doubt God. I knew He was real, but I certainly doubted myself and my own faith.

It was during this time that I discovered the writings of Isobel Kuhn, who was also a missionary in China under the China Inland Mission. Her writings did not solve my exhaustion problems, but they did calm down some of my feelings of panic over the exhaustion. She was practical and relatively simple in her approach, and that comforted me. Furthermore I began to see my life as an arena upon which how I behaved and what test I encountered would have value throughout all eternity. In short I found meaning in suffering.

Charles H. Spurgeon had been a common household name in my childhood, yet his writings only became significant to me in college. As a student I was fairly legalistic in my viewpoint on Christian truth. I was also zealous and yet I was compassionate too. Then I came across an article in His magazine on depression which contained material resurrected from some old sermons of Charles Spurgeon.

Charles Haddon Spurgeon, the "prince of preachers" in nineteenth-century England, had little hope to offer those who wished to eradicate depression. Yet because of his own periodic times of deep distress, he offered much good counsel on how to cope with and even positively use the problem of depression. I have read nothing since the writings of Spurgeon which, on a psychological and spiritual level, handles the subject more aptly.

In those student days, I saw for the first time that certain emotions such as fear or depression, so traditionally viewed as sin by many Christians, were not necessarily sin at all; but that our Lord himself went through great emotional pain in the Garden of Gethsemane. The more compassionate element of my personality was nurtured, which was to be a necessary step in growth if later I was to become a counselor dealing with people's emotions and pain.

F.B. Meyer and Geraldine Taylor, or Mrs. Howard Taylor as she is so often called in her books, were two writers who became important to me as a young adult, and ever since. As a teacher I found myself trying to be patient with unruly students, trying to love a school administrator who had been unfair with me, trying to forgive a friend who had let me down. Then I discovered that F.B. Meyer, Bible expositor and preacher in nineteenth century England, had something very important to say to me. God was not asking me to feel patience, or love, or forgiveness. He was asking me to act, not feel. I was to take His love, for example, and then act in love. The feelings would usually follow, later, but they were His responsibility, not mine. Another step in freedom in Christ had been taken, once again under the tutelege of one whom I would never know on this earth.

Geraldine Taylor, missionary to China and biographer of the China Inland Mission in those early days, had always influenced me from the time I could first understand the books and stories which she wrote. Yet because she rarely talked about herself in her books I was not aware of her as a person. She simply wrote about people who influenced me, like Hudson Taylor.

Then as a young adult I read her biography written by her niece, Joy Guinness. Because of my own struggle with over-extension, I related to her similar conflict. The letters from her father, along with her own comments, were of particular help to me in this area. Any final vestiges of legalism, spiritualization of fatigue, and tendencies toward making humanness into sin slipped off.

A week ago I spoke to Henry and Mary Guinness, Geraldine's nephew and his wife. They are elderly now, and Henry's memories are those of young schoolboy. Yet several things which were said were of great importance. Confirming Geraldine's life-long battle with over-extension, Mrs. Guinness told how when Geraldine was involved in the writing of a book, "Uncle Howard looked after her like everything so that she kept everything right, so that she would be able to have her quiet."[3]

According to Mr. Guinness, Geraldine was an exacting person regarding her work, but was also a very positive person. She was thoughtful and encouraging, and would often write little notes to people. She saw beauty in everything, so that others who may have shared in her experience often had a different story to tell. She saw the village with the stream going through it. Others may have only felt the heat and the dust.

Consistent with this positive viewpoint, according to both Mary and Henry Guinness, Geraldine lived in the daily expectation of the Lord's return. Still she took God's work on this earth as seriously as if He would not return for quite a long time.

As I thought over the main impression that Geraldine had made on my life, I realized that it was in the area of spiritual renewal. She over-worked, but then she recovered. She suffered, and then turned that suffering into blessing. She despaired, and then turned to God on an even deeper level.

When I asked Mr. Guinness if anything stood out in his memory relating to Geraldine, he basically remembered her as "just an aunt." But then he paused, and said that she frequently repeated one sentence: "Behold, I will do a new thing."[4] The statement confirmed my own impression. For to me that one saying pretty well sums up the life of Geraldine Guinness Taylor, Hudson Taylor's daughter-in-law.

Personally I will always have a special feeling of affection for Geraldine Taylor, until that day when I myself join that wonderful group of witnesses and, hopefully, spend time getting to know her better.

Thus the influence of this particular group of people has been woven into the fabric of my life since I was very small. In Hebrews twelve, verse one, we read of those saints who have gone on before:

> Wherefore seeing we also are compassed about with so great a cloud of witnesses, let us lay aside every weight, and the sin which doth so easily beset us, and let us run with patience the race that is set before us . . .

In writing to her children Amy Carmichael once said: "If this note is ever in your hands it will be because I am out of sight, with the Lord. But I shall not be forgetting you. I do not forget you now although I see you so seldom. I shall be thinking of you, loving you, praying for you, rejoicing as I see you run your race."

At another time she further explained: "Surely being with him will mean a new power to pray? It must, for to be present with the Lord must mean access in a far more vital sense than is possible now, and surely that will mean a new power to speak to him about our beloved?"

It is the belief of this writer that the words which these witnesses spoke in their lifetimes speak for themselves, without explanation. Perhaps because of their influence on my own personal life, I can serve as a bridge between this wealth of inspiration and teaching from the past and today's world as it edges into the twenty-first century. Now, too, they are a part of that living cloud of witnesses of Hebrews twelve which surround us.

One writer who is included in this book has influenced me as a living person rather than as a part of that great cloud of witnesses of the past. I first remember the Graham name from the summer of 1949. My parents, Uncle Blanton, and Aunts Esther, Ruth, and Lydia went to nearby Los Angeles to a huge tent with a sawdust floor and heard the new, upcoming evangelist, Billy Graham. The tent, the sawdust floor, and the image of a fiery young preacher stands out most in my memory. After that, fairly regular donations to the crusades and the receipt of books and literature in the mail from the Billy Graham Evangelistic Association were a part of our normal family life.

Later, as a not-sure-of-myself beginning writer, it was natural for me to send a first piece, a poem, to Decision magazine. To my surprise, they published it. They even paid for it! When I cashed my check at Sav-on drug store, the clerk laughed and said: "I thought people gave to Billy Graham instead of getting checks from him." Later on as I wrote some books for the publishing arm of the Graham organization I had occasion to interview Mrs. Graham on several occasions, and she, too, has made a permenant imprint on my life.

Ruth Bell Graham was born in China, of parents who were Presbyterian missionaries. From my talks with her as well as from her writings, and particularly her poems, I have found encouragement in the area of a day by day walk with God, making, as she puts it, "the least of all that goes and the most of all that comes."[5] Furthermore, because she is the only one of the people talked about in this book with whom I have had a personal encounter, beyond the words has been the reality of the life.

It is always scary to talk to someone whom you have read about in books. Usually it is better to stick with the books! To the contrary, I have never had a conversation with Mrs. Graham or received a note from her that has not left me feeling blessed. In her day by day walk with God she has a legacy of her own to leave to this century and those who come after.

The eight people who are written about in this book, as well as those who appear in the vignettes, have deeply influenced me. It is my prayer that God will take the dust of words and transform them by His Holy Spirit so that the lives and writings of these people will encourage and transform each person who is led to read this book.

> Take this book in Thy wounded hand,
>   Jesus, Lord of Calvary,
> Let it go forth at Thy command,
>   Use it as it pleaseth Thee.
>
> Dust of earth, but Thy dust, Lord,
>   Blade of grass in Thy Hand a sword,
> Nothing, nothing unless it be
>   Purged and quickened, O Lord, by Thee.

Amy Carmichael[6]

Frances Ridley Havergal

Born in England, Frances Ridley Havergal was a hymn writer as well as the author of devotional material which was quoted from by men like F.B. Meyer. Her most famous hymn may well be "Take my life and let it be Consecrated, Lord to Thee;..." A poem which appears in Geraldine Taylor's biography is virtually forgotten today but states beautifully the biblical view of the preciousness of life.

"The Best is Yet to Be"

"Just when Thou wilt—Thy time is best
Thou shalt appoint my hour of rest,
Marked by the Sun of perfect love,
Shining unchangeably above.

"Just when Thou wilt—no choice for me!
Life is a gift to use for Thee:
Death is a hushed and glorious tryst
With Thee, my King, my Saviour, Christ!"[1]

(1836–1879)

Her devotional writing, while less known than her hymns, emphasizes the theme of the Lordship of Christ. In *My King* she uses the image of the house to portray the position of the believer: "It is when the King has really come in peace to His own home in the 'contrite and humble spirit'...when He has entered in to make his abode there—that the soul is satisfied with Him alone...It all hinges upon Jesus coming into the heart as 'His *own* house,'...For if there are some rooms of which we do not give up the key, some little sitting room which we would like to keep as a little mental retreat, with a view from the window, which we do not quite want to give up— some lodger whom we would rather not send away just yet—some little dark closet which we have not resolution to open and set to rights—of course the King has not yet full possession; it is not all and really 'His own' ...Only throw open *all* the doors, 'and the King of Glory shall come in,' and then there will be no craving for other guests. He will 'fill this house with glory,' and there will be no place left for gloom."[2]

CHAPTER 4

F.B. Meyer: Putting Faith Into Shoeleather

S tanding at the gate of a prison, waiting to help a man who had just been released, nineteenth century preacher and Bible scholar F.B. Meyer watched man after man walk through the prison gates and cross the street to the closest Bar. Soon afterwards most of the men were back in the prison. The prison gates were like a revolving door, from the prison to the Bar and then back again.

The practical result in the life of Meyer was that each morning, for as long as he remained in Leicester, England, he met prisoners as they were released and invited them to a nearby Coffee House. There in the Coffee House this stately, scholarly man of God helped the former inmates make plans for their future and offered them concrete help.

On one particular occasion a certain man told Meyer that he could not accept help until he had fulfilled his vow to have one pint of ale on the morning of his freedom from prison. Nothing would persuade him otherwise. Rather than walking away in disgust, but preferring that the man himself stay away from the Bar, Meyer agreed to get him the ale if the ex-con would then promise to stay off liquor from that time on. This left Mr. Meyer with a dilemma of considerable proportions. Keep in mind that Meyer was a well known man by this time, easily recognizable in a public place. Says Meyer:

"I was in such a position that I did not dare to send any of the men who were at that time assisting me into the public house hard by to get that pint of porter: and I knew there was no one on the premises belonging to the coffee house company that I could employ for the purpose. And so, as there was nothing else to do, I caught up the first jug that was within reach and sallied forth to the public house at the opposite corner to get this pint of porter. I felt very strange. The barmaid who served me looked at me with such amazement that I think she supposed I had suddenly lost my reason. I assured her however that it was the final pint: and explained to her that it was not for myself but for a man in whom I was deeply interested.

"On arriving at my little breakfast party with the jug and glass in my hand, I poured the porter out as quietly as possible without the 'head' which porter drinkers are accustomed to appreciate. He took the glass and began to drink, and I gave such an unconscious groan that, after two or three efforts, he put down the remainder and said, 'This is the miserablest pint of porter I ever drank. Where's your card, sir? I may as well sign it as drink any more.'"[1]

The results of his work with released prisoners continued on after the time of F.B. Meyer, under the name of an organization. But Meyer himself had organized a window-washing and a wood-cutting business; he had set up a bank where the men could save money; and he had provided a place of housing as well. Signs in Leicester read: "F.B. Meyer-Firewood Merchant" and "F.B. Meyer-Window-Washing." Yet during all of this time he was still the pastor of Melbourne Hall.

Whether it was with prisoners, orphans, or ordinary people who were in trouble, throughout his life Meyer was the personification of charitable works, and no one who turned to him for help was denied that help. Yet the acts of charity were only vehicles by which, in part, he accomplished the greatest impact of his life: causing men and women to understand and live in the good of the Indwelling Christ.

These acts of Christian belief put into shoeleather attracted others to him and his message. His behavior validated the reality of the message of "Christ In Me." Through his good deeds, as well as in the volumes of sermons and books, he preached a sermon.

A little boy of ten was enrolled in a school in Leicester. Every day the child watched the stately-looking preacher walk away with two or three ex-cons. He saw them go together into the Welford Coffee House for "breakfast, a talk, and a fresh start in life." Continued the child, now grown into a man: "I went home one day and said, 'Mother, I wish when I grow up I could be a 'Meyer.' She asked me what I meant, and I told her how I loved the 'one' for what he did.

"'That "one" was you, sir,'" the man said in later years to Meyer. "'Last Christmas I visited the Leicester Gaol and recited to the fellows there...I suddenly thought of the boy of ten that I was, and swiftly it came to me that I was something of a "Meyer": the sermon has found its issue. I am— here.'"[2]

The man went on to tell Meyer that because of his sermon preached in shoeleather, as the ten year old boy had watched the great man of God come before dawn to the prison and lead these men, one by one, to a better life, that ten year old had grown to a man who became in his own a way a "Meyer" and in so doing ministered to over 250,000 men in France and elsewhere. "Please receive my thanks"[3] he said to Meyer.

Born on April 8, 1847, F.B. Meyer died at the age of eighty-two on March 28, 1929. During his lifetime he was a preacher in England at the same time that the popular G. Campbell Morgan and Charles Haddon Spurgeon occupied pulpits nearby. From the visits of D.L. Moody he learned the art of winning men and women to Christ. Later in his pastorate at Christ Church in London, when he felt in danger of burning out, the great Bible expositor A.T. Pierson took his place. Indeed he seemed to live at a time of the spiritual greats. He was close friends with Dr. Grattan Guinness who was influencial in missions, and who was the father of Geraldine Guinness Taylor, Hudson Taylor's daughter-in-law. The principles upon which the China Inland Mission was founded were in agreement with the beliefs of F.B. Meyer, and so it was not surprising that Hudson Taylor and he were also very close friends.

When he was five F.B. Meyer prayed: "Put Thy Holy Spirit in me to make my heart good, like Jesus Christ was."[4] After that day, he prayed the same prayer every day. On the day before he died he was asked if he had any new vision of his Saviour. He answered, "No, just the constant interchange between Him and me."[5] Says his biographer W.Y. Fullerton, "Between those two experiences his whole life was included...Christ and he were well known to each other."[6] The word interchange sums up the thrust of Meyer's message better than any other. To him the Christ life was just that: the constant interchange of "Christ in Me," His life for my life, His life lived out from my life.

My first recollection of the influence of F.B. Meyer in my own life was when I was a young school teacher, trying desperately to live the life of a

Christian in witness to my high school students. I was trying to live the
Christian life and was constantly discouraged by my own efforts. Then I
read something from F.B. Meyer which changed my whole outlook.

> "It was first taught me by a grey-haired clergyman," explained Meyer, "in
> the study of the Deanery, at Southampton. Once, when tempted to feel
> great irritation, he told us that he looked up and claimed the patience and
> gentleness of Christ; and since then it had become the practice of his life to
> claim from Him the virtue of which he felt the deficiency in himself. In
> hours of unrest, 'Thy Peace, Lord.' In hours of irritation, 'Thy Patience,
> Lord.' In hours of temptation, 'Thy Purity, Lord.' In hours of weakness,
> 'Thy Strength, Lord.' It was to me a message straight from the throne. Till
> then I had been content with ridding myself with burdens; now I began to
> reach forth to positive blessing"...7

The idea of exchanging my life for the life of Christ reminded me of the
tremendous impact which Hudson Taylor had made on my life as a teenger.
Apparently Hudson Taylor influenced F.B. Meyer in the same way. Meyer
describes his first meeting with Taylor:

> "I remember so well Hudson Taylor coming to my church the first time I
> ever met him. He stepped on the platform and opened the Bible to give an
> address, and said, 'Friends, I will give you the motto of my life,' and he
> turned to Mark 11:22: 'Have faith in God.' The margin says,'Have the faith
> of God,' but Hudson Taylor said it meant, 'Reckon on God's faith to you.'
> He continued, 'All my life has been so fickle. Sometimes I could trust,
> sometimes I could not, but when I could not trust then I reckoned that God
> would be faithful.' There is a text that says, 'If we believe not, yet He
> abideth faithfull, He cannot deny Himself.' And sometimes I go to God
> about a thing, and say, 'My God, I really cannot trust Thee about this, I can-
> not trust Thee to pull me through this expenditure of money with my
> means, but I reckon on Thy faithfulness.' And when you cease to think
> about your faith, and like Sarah, reckon Him faithful, your faith comes
> without your knowing it, and you are strong."8

Quoting another man of God on the same topic of "Christ in Me," Meyer further illustrates the point:

> "They tell me that George Macdonald, wanting to teach his children honor
> and truth and trust, places on the mantel-shelf of the common room in their
> house, money enough for the whole use of his family. If the wife wants

money she goes for it, if the boys and girls want money they go for it; whatever want there is in that house is supplied from that mantel-shelf deposit. So God put in Jesus everything the soul can want, and He says, 'Go and take it. It is all there for you.'"9

In a still further explanation of the words "Christ in Me," Meyer says: "These are two great words—*claim* God's fulness, and *reckon* that whatever you can claim is yours, although no answering emotion assures you that it is. Dare to act in faith, stepping out in the assurance that you have just what you have claimed, and doing just as you would do it if you *felt* to have it."10

Futhermore, claims Meyer:

"...if the gifts sought from the Father's hands are really such as He can bestow, there should be no need for the incessant repetition of the same requests because they would be claimed and taken from His outstretched hand. A Christian will request prayer that he may receive a certain grace of Christian character; whereas there is not the least reason in the world why he should not take as much of it as he requires, altogether apart from the intercession of others. We ask for health, or power, or deliverance, or vindication, with the accent of weary uncertainty, which proffers the same request, year after year, regardless of the voice, which is ever crying, 'Whosoever will, let him take freely.'"11

In essense, "The weakest man who knows God is strong to do exploits. All the might of God awaits the disposal of our faith. As a child by touching a button may set in motion a mighty steamship, making it glide like a swan into her native element, so a stripling who has learned to reckon on God may bring the whole forces of Deity to bear on men and things on the world's battlefield."12 "We must always add His resources to our own, when making our calculations."13

For all of his godliness, F.B. Meyer had his own flesh and blood struggles and irritations. When the great evangelist D.L. Moody came to England, Meyer and Moody became close friends. Yet he was less enthusiatic about Moody's singing companion, Sankey, even though Moody owed a great deal of his success to the efforts of Sankey. In all fairness to Meyer, solo singing in a service was an American invention and was still considered by many to be irreverent. Years later Meyer wrote, with some validity, I believe: "It is certain that solo and anthem singing may become a grest snare to spiritual worship unless the choir leader and organist are distinctly spiritual people."14 Still, not all of his attitude was based on conviction alone. Before a meeting in Canada he was heard to pray: "Help me to be patient while the choir sings, and let them not distract the people from the message we want them to get."[15]

At another point in Meyer's life, when Dr. G. Campbell Morgan commanded large audiences while Meyer's devotional sermons were more sparsely attended, Meyer reportedly confided to a friend: "The only way I can conquer my feelings is to pray for him daily, which I do."[16]

Perhaps part of his practical emphasis on the everyday problems of life arose from the fact that his own life seemed to be one of ordinary greatness. He was an extraordinary man with an extraordinary ministry. Yet in his personal life he did not seem to have the catastrophic incidents of a Hudson Taylor or the ongoing depression of a Spurgeon. Still, while the lack of trauma did not seem to lessen his insight into pain or his sensitivity to the suffering of those around him, it did, perhaps, help make him more objectively helpful.

> "One afternoon in a tram-car in North London, he noticed on the opposite seat an elderly woman with a basket, evidently a charwoman returning from her day's work. She appeared to be anything but happy, and as the car emptied only he and she were left. Then, having recognized him all along, she summoned up courage to speak to him and calling him by name, she told him her story. As a widow she had been left alone in the world except for her crippled daughter who, in spite of her affliction, was a continual joy to her. Every morning, as she explained, when she came home from her work she knew her daughter was in the room where they lived, ready to greet her. She was always there, and at night in the darkness she could stretch out her hand and know she was there, too. She made tea in the morning, and left her for the day, but she knew all the time that her daughter was there to greet her with a glad face when she returned. 'And now,' she said sadly, 'now she is dead, and I am alone, and I am miserable: I am going home, and it is scarcely home, for she is not there.'
>
> "There was little time for discussion, but Meyer was 'At Attention!' for his Master on the moment. 'When you get home and put the key in the door,' he said, 'say aloud, "Jesus, I know You are here," and be ready to greet Him directly when you open the door. And as you light the fire tell Him what has happened during the day; if anybody has been kind, tell Him, if anybody has been unkind, tell Him, just as you would have told your daughter. Be sure to make your cup of tea. At night stretch out your hand in the darkness and say, "Jesus, I know you are here."' Then the tram-car reached the terminus, and they parted.[17]

A few months later F.B. Meyer was on the same tram-car again. A woman greeted him. "'You don't know me, Mr. Meyer,' she said. 'I am afraid I do not,' he replied. Then she reminded him of the interview some months before. 'But you are not the same woman,' he said in astonishment. 'Oh, yes, I am,' she said. 'I did as you told me. I went home and said, "Jesus, I know You are here," and I kept saying it, and it has made all the difference in my life, and now I feel I know Him.'"[18]

For all of his practical emphasis and understanding of everyday life, F.B. Meyer was still a scholar, a brilliant thinker, and a prolific writer. His legacy to the Church of more than fifty books includes two autobiographical volumes, thirteen books on great men of the Bible, and more than twenty devotional volumes. His greatest contribution is probably the large number of excellent Bible commentaries which he wrote. I have found these commentaries to be of particular value since, not only do they explain various biblical passages, they possess a devotional quality which never fails to bless. They are not just dry commentary; they are living words.

If his theology was practical, however, it was a practicality which grew from an ability to distill the simple out of the profound. I have found that it is always easier to make a difficult truth clear to others when you understand it first in its most complex form. In both the writings and the sermons of Meyer the truth of exchanging the life of Christ for our own life is stated simply, but with biblical foundations which are sound and deep in their truth.

While I was reading the writings of F.B. Meyer in order to write this book I discovered a book published in 1896, inscribed to my maternal grandfather, Alfred Benson, from my Aunts Esther and Ruth. The volume is carefully marked in pencil by my grandfather, markings which point out Meyer's depth of teaching with relationship to the indwelling Christ. Yet many of these words fit our times as we move into the twenty-first century even more than they applied to the end of the nineteenth century.

Setting the stage for the possibility of true recovery from the bondage of addiction, memories of past grievances, and habit patterns which enslave, Meyer says: "We reverse the Divine order. We say, feeling, Faith, fact. God says, fact, Faith, feeling. With Him feeling is of small account—He only asks us to be willing to accept His own Word, and to cling to it because He has spoken it, in entire disregard of what we may feel."[19]

Then, stating the theological base for the practical theology of recovery, good spiritual growth, and the best of psychological treatment, Meyer explains:

> "'Master, where dwellest Thou?' they asked of old. And in reply, Jesus led them from the crowded Jordan bank to the slight tabernacle of woven osiers where He temporarily lodged. But if we address the same question to Him now, He will point, not to the lofty dome of heaven, not to the splendid structure of stone or marble, but to the happy spirit that loves, trusts, and obeys Him. 'Behold,' saith He, 'I stand at the door and knock. If any man hear my voice, and open the door, I will come into him.' 'We will come,' He said, including His Father with Himself, 'and make our abode with him.' He promised to be within each believer as a tenant in a house; as sap in the branch; as life-blood and life-energy in each member, however feeble, of the body."[20]

It is true, continues Meyer, that

> "the heavens…with all their light and glory alone seem worthy of Him. But even there He is not more at home than He is with the humble and contrite spirit that simply trusts in Him…But there is a reason why many whose natures are certainly the temple of Christ, remain ignorant of the presence of the wonderful Tenant that sojourns within. *He dwells so deep.* Below the life of the body, which is as the curtain of the tent; below the life of the soul, where thought and feeling, judgment and imagination, hope and love, go to and fro, ministering as white-stoled priests in the holy place; below the play of light and shade, resolution and will, memory and hope, the perpetual ebb and flow of the tides of self-consciousness, there, through the Holy Spirit, Christ dwells, as of old the Shechinah dwelt in the Most Holy Place, closely shrouded from the view of man."

> "It is comparatively seldom that we go into these deeper departments of our being. We are content to live the superficial life of sense. We eat, we drink, we sleep; we give ourselves to enjoy the lust of the flesh, the lust of the eyes, and the pride of life; we fulfill the desires of the flesh and of the mind. Or we abandon ourselves to the pursuit of knowledge and culture, of science and art; we reason, speculate, argue; we make short excursions into the realm of morals, that sense of right and wrong which is part of the make-up of men. But we have too slight an acquaintance with the deeper and more mysterious chamber of the spirit. Now this is why the majority of believers are so insensible of their Divine and wonderful Resident, who makes the regenerated spirit His abode."[21]

With that sense of balance which so characterizes the ministry of Meyer, he speaks of the indwelling work of the Holy Spirit in a way which is soundly biblical and yet does not minimize, as some do, the work of that One who is, after all, *God* the Spirit. With characteristic depth and simplicity combined, Meyer explains:

> "I am not anxious here to distinguish between the filling of the Holy Ghost and the baptism of fire. So far as I can understand it, they are synonymous." Still, warns Meyer: "Say not that this filling by the Spirit was for the first Christians and not for us. Certainly His gifts were part of the special machinery needed to impress the Gentile world; but the filling of the Spirit is conterminous with no one age. Alas! that many think that the Almighty, like some bankrupt builder, constructed the portico of His Church with marble, and has finished it with common brick!"[22]

In a more complete explanation Meyer adds:

> "It is of course true that the Holy Ghost is the sole agent in conversion, becoming the occupant of the temple, which is presented to Him by the nature of man (I Cor. vi. 19). And it is equally clear that the Holy Spirit as a person enters the newly regenerated heart. But there is a vast difference between having the Holy Ghost and being filled by Him. In the one case, He may be compared to a mighty man that cannot save, relegated to an obscure corner of the heart, whilst the larger part of the nature is excluded from His gracious influences. In the other, He is a welcome guest, to whom every part of the being is thrown open, and who pervades it with the freedom of the balmy air of summer, sweeping through open windows, breathing through long corridors, and carrying into further recesses the fragrance of a thousand flowers.

> "There are a great many Christians who undoubtedly received the Holy Spirit at the earliest moment of faith; indeed, their faith is the result of His work; but they have never gone further; they have never yielded their whole nature to His indwelling; they have had no further experience of His Pentecostal Filling."[23]

Yet there is a danger in measuring one's spiritual life by emotion. In speaking of the Spirit of God dwelling within him, Meyer cautions: "…as I had received Him without emotion, I might expect ever to retain and enlarge its measure, whether the song-birds of summer or the stillness of winter occupied my heart."[24]

Of the result of Christ living in me, by the power of the indwelling Spirit, Meyer summarizes: "It is like a poor man having a millionaire friend come to live with him."[25] Yet "Christ in Me" does not mean that we get everything we want, or that we never suffer. On the other hand, it is the opposite of the me-ism of our day which depends upon the impoverished resources of *me*. To the contrary it means that Christ is Lord. It means that "He never leads us through a place too narrow for Him to pass as well.[26] It means that the believer is "enclosed in the invisible film of the Divine Presence, as a far-traveled letter in the envelope which protects it from hurt and soil."[27]

For those who spiritualize emotional pain, and for those who mistakenly feel that unless they are happy all the time they are sinning, Meyer warns once again that:

> "*Emotion is no true test of our spiritual state.* Rightness of heart often shows itself in gladness of heart, just as bodily health generally reveals itself in exuberant spirits. But it is not always so. In other words, absence of joy does not always prove that the heart is wrong…Perhaps the nervous system, may have been overtaxed, as Elijah's was in the wilderness, when, after the long strain of Carmel and his flight was over, he lay down upon the sand and asked to die—a request which God met, not with a rebuke, but with food and sleep. Perhaps the Lord has withdrawn the light from the landscape in order to see whether He was loved for Himself or merely for His gifts…Somber colors become the tried and suffering soul."[28]

F.B. Meyer, like Charles Spurgeon and James Fraser, would have understood the concept of burnout, for burnout is the ever-present enemy of many who try to serve God, and far too often it is mistaken for godliness. Said Meyer: "True holiness does not consist in bare walls, and hard seats, and a dingy environment; but in all that resembles God's work in nature, which is exquisitely beautiful…" Likewise, "It is not wrong to unbend the bow in manly games, that develop the sinews and expand the lungs, or to join in the pastimes of your age and companions, so long as you can write on bat and football, on tennis racquet and piano, on oar and paddle, on skate or sleigh, the words…*Holiness to the Lord*."[29]

Consistent with his viewpoint on depression and burnout, F.B. Meyer combined a rare mixture of holiness and compassion which showed itself in how he dealt with the severe tests of life as well as in with the trivial. A woman who often typed for Meyer lost two of his articles. In a note to her he wrote: "I can imagine your distress. Think no more of it and we will halve the loss. I think it was a good thing, as my second attempt was an improvement.[30]

On a less traumatic level, in writing of his dog he once said: "...he used to worry me very much to be fed at dinner, but he never got any food that way. But lately he has adopted something which always conquers me; he sits under the table, and puts one paw on my knee. He never barks, never leaps around, never worries me, but he sits under the table with that one paw on my knee, and that conquers me; I cannot resist the appeal. Although my wife says I must never do it, I keep putting little morsels under the table."[31] One cannot help but feel affection for this man who was so human, while at the same time he was so filled with the Divine.

Meyer combined righteousness with a winsome tenderness, a quality aptly called "velvet steel" by Warren W. Wiersbe, who took the term from Carl Sandberg's description of Abraham Lincoln. Nowhere is this quality more apparent than in Meyer's dealing with sin: "You may talk of chastisement or correction, for our Father deals with us as with sons; or you may speak of reaping the results of mistakes and sins dropped as seeds into life's furrows in former years; or you may have to bear the consequences of the sins and mistakes of others; but do not speak of punishment. Surely all the guilt and penalty of sin were laid on Jesus, and he put them away forever... if He once began to punish us, life would be too short for the infliction of all that we deserve. Besides, how could we explain the anomalies of life, and the heavy sufferings of the saints as compared with the gay life of the ungodly? Surely, if our sufferings were penal, there would be a reversal of these lots."[32]

Rather than place blame for suffering, Meyer saw suffering as having meaning and purpose and in that sense as something to be used for God. His advice was: "Wait, till ten years are past. I warrant thee, that in that time thou wilt find some, perhaps ten, afflicted as thou art...Thou wilt bless God that thou wert able to comfort others with the comfort wherewith thou thyself hadst been comforted of God..." Then with his ever-present sense of the practical, Meyer gently reminds us to "remember to store up an accurate remembrance of the way in which God comforts thee."[33] He reminds us never to waste suffering.

With rare sensitivity to the inner longing and disappointment of those who have at some time wanted to serve God in a specific ministry and then were thwarted, he reminds them in words reminiscent of the writings of English poet Robert Browning, or the American poet James R. Lowell, that all they aspired to be counts with God. Says Meyer: "The picture which is to gain immortality is always to be painted; the book which is to elucidate the problem of the ages is always to be written; the immortal song is always to be sung. The young man is kept at his desk in the counting-house instead of going to the pulpit; the girl becomes a withered woman, cherishing a faded flower; the king hands on to his son the building of the house..."[34]

Referring to Solomon, regarding God's decision *not* to let David build the temple: "'The Lord said unto David my father, Whereas it was in thine heart to build a house for my name, thou didst well that it was in thine heart.' David was a better man because he had given expression to the noble purpose. Its gleam left a permanent glow on his life. The rejected candidate to the missionary society stands upon a higher moral platform than those who were never touched by the glow of missionary enthusiasm. For a woman to have loved passionately, even though the dark waters may have engulfed her love before it was consummated, leaves her ever after richer, deeper, than if she had never loved, nor been loved in return...Thou didst well that it was in thine heart....God will credit us with what we would have been if we might...No true ideals are fruitless; somehow they help the world of men. No tears are wept, no prayers uttered, no conceptions honestly entertained in vain..." And always, "somehow God makes up to us."[35] God is no man's debtor.

When I was a year out of college, a friend of mine who was the same age as I died from a lingering disease. Shortly before she died she said: "I wish I could have lived longer in order to serve God more." The words have been with me all these years.

My Aunt Lydia didn't die young but she did spend her life in an office job when what she really wanted to do was go to the mission field like her sister, my Aunt Ruth. She had a special burden for South America, and she even pursued a study of the Spanish language. But Aunt Lydia felt it was wrong to leave her aged mother, and so she stayed home. In later years she became the caretaker for several other family members, including my Aunt Ruth, once she had returned from China.

My young friend and my Aunt Lydia would have been encouraged by the words of Meyer. Perhaps my aunt was actually uplifted by them since many of Meyer's books which I am using came to me from my family. And I am sure that in the economy of Heaven, their aspirations have been rewarded, and they have also shared in the reward of the work of those Christian workers for whom they secretly prayed.

God was a real Person to F.B. Meyer. His enablement, demands, comfort, priorities, and joy pervaded every area of Meyer's life. It is consistent with that reality that angels, too, were realized as actual beings; and Heaven was felt as a real place. Meyer manages to convey that reality to his reader.

In a striking example Meyer tells of a pastor who had made an ardent enemy of a man by rebuking him for his sin. The man vowed revenge. "One night the pastor was called to visit a house that could only be reached by passing over a plank which bridged an impetuous torrent. Nothing seemed easier to his enemy than to conceal himself on the bank till the man of God was returning from the opposite end of the plank, to meet him in the middle, throw him into the deep and turbid stream, leaving it to be surmised that in the darkness he had simply lost his foothold. When, however, from his hiding-place he caught sight of the pastor's figure in the dim light, he was surprised to see that he was not alone, but accompanied by another. There were two figures advancing toward him across the narrow plank, and he did not dare attempt his murderous deed. And as they passed his hiding place, the one whom he did not know cast such a glance toward him as convinced him of the sinfulness of the act he had contemplated, and began a work in his heart which led to his conversion."

After his conversion, the would-be assassin confronted the pastor and told him of his murderous intention. "It would have been your death had you not been accompanied," he said. "What do you mean?" replied the pastor. "I was absolutely alone." "'Nay,' said he, 'there were two.' Then the pastor knew that God had sent His angel…"[36]

Always, with Meyer, there is perfect balance, even in dealing with such a topic as the balance between that which angels may be asked to do and that which only God Himself does: "He may give His angels charge concerning us when we are in danger; but He keeps our purification beneath His special superintendence…what a comfort it is that He surrenders this work to no other hands than His own…"[37]

But if angels were real beings to Meyer, Heaven was equally a real place to be looked forward to. Of that transition to Heaven, death, Meyer speaks with comfort: "Obviously, in death there is no break in the soul's consciousness. The life of the spirit is altogether independent of the body in which it dwells. The signal-box may be in ruins, and yet the operator may be within—as clear in thought and quick of hand as in the day when all was new."

In a statement which should subdue any Christian who contemplates suicide or Euthanasia, Meyer explains: "It often happens, when the body is at the point of death, that the spirit reveals itself in undiminished splendor, and flashes forth in thoughts that can never be forgotten, and words that can never die. And does not this prove, beyond doubt, that the spirit is only a lodger in the body, and when the house of its tabernacle is broken up, it is not affected, but simply passes out to find some other and more lasting home. 'We know that if the earthly house of our tabernacle' (this bodily frame) 'be dissolved, we have a house not made with hands, eternal, in the heavens' (2 Cor. v.1).

Continues Meyer: "There is no shadow of warrant for the idea (held by some) that there is a pause in our consciousness, between death and the resurrection. 'To depart,' said St. Paul, 'is to be with Christ, which is far better' (Phil. i. 25). But surely it could not have been far better to pass into a sort of sleep! Better to live on in this mortal life, amid the acutest sufferings, and to have the presence of Christ, than to lose that presence during centuries of unconsciousness."[38]

Concludes Meyer: *The moment of absence is the moment of presence.* As the spirit withdraws itself from the body, closing blinds and shutters as it retires, it immediately presents itself in the presence of the King, to go no more out for ever…Death is not a state, but an act; not a condition, but a passage. In this it finds its true analogy in birth, by which we entered upon a new stage of existence…A moment's anguish; a wrench; a step; a transition; a breaking through the thin veil, which hangs between two worlds; a stepping across the boundary line…And the soul carries with it across that boundary line its freight of thought and life, to pursue its continuity of being and love and purpose in an unbroken and uninterrupted course…"[39]

In a way which reminds me of Lewis's description of Heaven in the last Narnia book, where good things which are enjoyable on earth are even more enjoyable in Heaven, Meyer speaks of the actual place of Heaven with loving familiarity. To friends he wrote with delightful detail: "You dear souls! I do love you, and we must have a thousand years in Heaven. Let us meet at the middle gate on the Eastern aspect of the city, and then a picnic amid the Fountain of Waters."[40]

Then, right before his death, as he perhaps had a more distinct view of that Place to which he was soon going, he wrote to his physician and friend: "…we will ask that yonder our mansions may be together…" And, "…this a.m. it has been my request to 'the Prince' that He would allow our mansions to be simple, but situated side by side. I seem to understand that there have been so many arrivals lately that the angels have been set to make a new road, along the River Bank. I said that we should prefer this—so they are preparing two for us."[41]

Fanciful? A little. But one senses in these words the reality of a life lived with Jesus Christ, not the delusions of an unbalanced mind. Indeed, words written to his church a short time later, the last before his death, breathe sanity: "The love of God, the Grace of Christ our Lord, and the annointing, quickening and empowering grace of the Holy Spirit be with you all."[42]

In reading from many of the fifty volumes of F.B. Meyer, I have felt uplifted by the reality and yet practical balance from which he speaks. So much so, that I, too, would like to have a mansion somewhere in the vicinity of Meyer and all of the other great heroes of this book, as well as near that great body of family and friends of mine who already live in the Celestial City. It wouldn't have to be a big mansion, but something larger than I have now, a place, perhaps, where everyone who comes would fit! A River Bank appeals to me, too, and perhaps a few mountains and trees.

Early on in his ministry, before he sailed for his first visit to America, F.B. Meyer reassured his own church with words, spoken in the pulpit: "You can do without me: you cannot do without God." Says Fullerton: "That is the great service he did for the innumerable company of which I am but one—he linked us to God."[43]

Handley C.G. Moule

"Fellow and Dean of Trinity College, Cambridge, Lord Bishop of Durham, Teacher, Bible Expositor, Bishop Moule is my personal favorite of Bible Commentators," says Amy Carmichael.

"Sometimes, when we are distressed by past failure and tormented by fear of failure in the future should we again set our faces toward Jerusalem, nothing helps so much as to give some familiar Scripture time to enter into us and become part of our being. The words 'Grace for grace' have been a help to me since I read in a little old book of Bishop Moule's something that opened their meaning. (Till then I had not understood them.)

He says 'for' means simply instead.

'The image is of a perpetual succession of supply; a displacement ever going on; ceaseless changes of need and demand.

'The picture before us is as of a river. Stand on its banks, and contemplate the flow of waters. A minute passes, and another. Is it the same stream still? Yes. But is it the same water? No. The liquid mass that passed you a few

(1841–1920)

seconds ago fills now another section of the channel; new water has displaced it, or if you please replaced it; water instead of water. And so hour by hour, and year by year, and century by century, the process holds; one stream, other waters, living not stagnant, because always in the great identity there is perpetual exchange. Grace takes the place of grace;' (Love takes the place of love) 'ever new, ever old, ever the same, ever fresh and young, for hour by hour, for year by year, through Christ.'"[1]

"A letter, slipped into a book by mistake less than twenty years ago, has lately reappeared as such things kindly do sometimes. It was written from Auckland Castle soon after Mrs. Moule's death had left the Bishop very lonely, for his daughter Tesie had died a little while before, and his only other child was married. He writes of comfort 'dropt like an anodyne from the hand of the Physician into my great wound. (He gives no anaesthetics, but He does give anodynes.) I bless Him who is more near and dear to me than ever, in His mercy. My beloved one is not far from me. And I bless her Lord for calling her to go upstairs, and meet Him there, and our Tesie with Him, and for trusting me to meet the solitude here, and to find Him very near in it.'"[2]

CHAPTER 5

Amy Carmichael: Triumph In Suffering

O n a dull Sunday morning in Belfast, a young girl walked home from a fashionable church and encountered a pathetic old woman carrying a heavy bundle. Impulsively the girl helped her. Then, with horror, she thought that "respectable" people might see her. It was a moment of decision. In her mind flashed the words: "Gold, silver, precious stones, wood, hay, stubble. If any man's work abide..." (1 Corinthians 3:12,14). She looked around her and everything seemed normal. But, said Amy Carmichael later, "I knew that something had happened that had changed life's values. Nothing could ever matter again but the things that were eternal."[1]

Nothing Matters But That Which Is Eternal

Woven throughout her writings, "Nothing is important but that which is eternal," remains a theme carried out in practical terms with family relationships, friendships, or something as deep as illness and death. It is a principle which casts a new and vital perspective on how each of us lives.

In a fast-changing society with fluctuating values we may find it difficult to know what it means to live under God's approval. "God can't love me. I'm no good," said one lady sadly as she sat down in my office and poured out her feelings of self-hate. Another young woman refused much needed psychological help because she "can get all she needs from reading the Bible."

This woman, too, suffered from a deep sense of self hate; and she feared that if she sought counseling God would condemn her for not trusting Him enough. It hadn't occurred to her that God might actually use the counseling to help her put biblical principles into shoeleather.

At the advice of his pastor a young man brought his child to see me; He admitted that his real reason for coming was to talk about his extramarital affair—an affair of which the pastor had no knowledge and which, apart from being discovered, did not on the surface disturb the young man. When I asked him how he reconciled his sexual activity with his biblical knowledge, he replied, "I don't try to."

Apart from God, the confusion only deepens. In the 1992 Los Angeles riots a woman was seen sending her four year old daughter into a store to loot while she stayed outside. When a reporter asked another woman why she was stealing from the store if she knew it was wrong, the woman replied: "It's wrong, but everyone's doing it so it must be okay."

In the midst of such obvious confusion in a society which changes so fast that even Christians lose a perspective as to what God wants, Amy Carmichael offers an old but continuingly current point of view. Like the rest of us, she struggled to learn what God wanted of her. From that early moment in Belfast to the last years of total invalidism, she fought to know God's approval, and in the process gives us a believable example of dealing with suffering.

After a physical breakdown when she was a missionary in Japan, Amy Carmichael became a missionary in south India, rescuing children sold to the gods as temple prostitutes. There she actually took on Indian citizenship and melted into the Indian culture. Her goal was to do her work as Christ had done his on this earth.

In 1919, when she was awarded a high honor and was presented with a medal from the governor of Madras, she almost refused it. "It troubles me," she said, "to have an experience so different from His who was despised and rejected—not kindly honored."[2]

Miss Carmichael's standards were high. She insisted upon the children being raised with the highest standards of honesty and loyalty. That the Dohnavur Fellowship of India still exists is evidence that her standards were not so high, however, as to be spiritually unrealistic. That she could be very practical was evidenced in her long journeys on hot dusty roads to rescue an ill child. At the root of all her endeavors and in the midst of all her suffering was a deep desire to live under God's approval in all circumstances. Perhaps her attitude toward life can be summarized in one of her poems, "Make Me Thy Fuel."

From prayer that asks that I may be
Sheltered from winds that beat on Thee,
From fearing when I should aspire,
From faltering when I should climb higher.
From silken self, O Captain, free
Thy soldier who would follow Thee.

From subtle love of softening things,
From easy choices, weakenings,
Not thus are spirits fortified,
Not this way went the Crucified,
From all that dims Thy Calvary,
O Lamb of God, deliver me.

Give me the love that leads the way
The faith that nothing can dismay,
The hope no disappointments tire.
The passion that will burn like fire,
Let me not sink to be a clod;
Make me Thy fuel, Flame of God.[3]

The problem of God's approval becomes even more complicated when suffering is involved. Perhaps one of the toughest issues that a thinking person faces—and certainly a psychotherapist who witnesses daily the inner torture of so many—is the problem of pain. Nietzsche has quite accurately stated that "he who knows the *why* to his existence can endure any *how*."

Sometimes the how hurts so badly that the *why* is hard to remember. It is hard for a small child to work for eight years to walk. The *how* seems too tedious and painful; the *why* feels remote and at times seemingly unattainable. And sometimes the *why* becomes obscure or is unknowable to finite minds. Why do people starve to death or nearly starve? Why do little children at age three need therapy for emotional problems so deeply engrained that scars remain for life? Why, on a human level, does life seem so much more filled with pain than pleasure, with mere survival as a primary goal for many?

In her various books Amy Carmichael commented on different aspects of human suffering. In so doing she cast a meaning and a purpose on even the severest difficulties of life which is strengthening as well as enlightening.

Frequently, Christians who try to live in the light of eternity have severe doubts about their ability to do so. We know that we should love, but we find it difficult to love the unlovable. We fear failure and criticism, especially when we suffer and are criticized. Amy Carmichael described this well when she wrote: "Some are wonderfully created. They can go through a thick flight of stinging arrows and hardly feel them. It is as if they were clad in fine chain-armour.

"Others are made differently. The arrows pierce, and most sharply if they be shot by friends. The very tone of a voice can depress such a one for a week. (It can uplift, too; for the heart that is open to hurt is also very open to love.)

"The Indian [referring to the native of India] has by nature no chain-armour, and some of us can understand just what that means. But if we are to be God's knights, we must learn to go through flights of arrows, and so the teaching which was set on fashioning warriors, not weaklings, often dealt with this."[4] Again, Miss Carmichael's emphasis here is not on the eradication of suffering, but on the Christian ability to cope with it.

Triumph in Misunderstanding

The principle upon which Amy Carmichael operated under criticism is reflected in two of her illustrations: "Walker of Tinnevelly sat alone in his study reading the copy of a document addressed to the Archbishop of Canterbury. It was a petition against him and one or two other true men who had stood by him in his efforts to cut certain cankers out of this South Indian Church. It was an amazing composition, cruel and false because so ignorant.

"Walker came out from his study that day looking very white, and his eyes were like dark fires. But he went straight on like a man walking through cobwebs stretched across his path. And what does it matter now? He has seen his Lord's face. *All that troubles is only for a moment. Nothing is important but that which is eternal.*"[5]

In another instance Miss Carmichael spoke of her own experience in a setting where alcohol was forbidden to a "good Christian" and she was misrepresented in her presentation of the subject: "One of the first meetings she was asked to take in India was for English soldiers belonging to a South Indian cantonment. It was supposed to be a Temperance meeting, but Temperance was hardly mentioned. The soldiers needed something that went much deeper. That meeting was reported in the Parish magazine. An address had been given on the benefits of alcohol. It had come as a pleasant surprise, the writer said, to hear from a missionary that alcohol was beneficial.

"For a minute a quite young missionary felt this rather staggering. And then suddenly the thought came, 'It won't matter fifty years hence, so what does it matter now?' Nothing is important but that which is eternal."[6] So often it was the principle of viewing life in an eternal perspective which enabled Amy Carmichael to cope with suffering.

In my work as a counselor I see many who feel hurt from unjust criticism; for the idleness and, indeed, savagery of words can be felt as a very deep form of suffering. But perhaps those who feel the most criticism at times are those who are in positions of power, particularly in Christian work. A leader in the Christian world is troubled by a disturbed child. Instead of being upheld he is often criticized by fellow Christians. Illness is regarded as lack of faith in some circles. Men earnestly helping with the emotional problems of their congregation find themselves suddenly accused of a sexual affair. For such, the words "nothing matters but that which is eternal" is at times the only effective antidote.

Living Above Physical Illness

In speaking of another form of suffering—chronic physical pain—Amy Carmichael recounted this instance: "One of our Indian Viceroys, perhaps the most dazzling figure of them all, could not stand to face an audience without the support of a steel device, 'I, at times, suffer terribly from my back,' he wrote from out of the blaze of public life, 'and one day it will finish me. But so long as one is marching, I say, let the drums beat and the flags fly.' (Not many knew of that gnawing pain. Perhaps if it were remembered that often there is sackcloth under royal robes, the judgment of the world would be kinder.)

"Whatever the Iron Crown may be, so long as one is marching let the drums beat and the flags fly. What does it matter that no one knows the cost of those brave words? He whose crown was of thorns knows all that is covered from casual glance of man. Where others see merely a decorous exterior, He sees a soul, sometimes a tortured soul, looking up into His eyes for courage and grace to live triumphantly a moment at a time. And if we could hear spiritual voices speak, we should hear something like this, 'Thy flesh and thy heart faileth? I know, my child, I know. But I am the strength of thy heart and thy portion for ever. Thou shalt not be forgotten of Me.'"[7]

Those who are well are sometimes not able to understand and accept those who are ill. As one patient said to me, "If my friend is sick I'm sorry; but she's going to have to forget her illness and go back to work. After all, her rent has to be paid." Or worse still was the comment directed to a young girl who was told that she was in braces only because she didn't have enough faith.

Miss Carmichael showed profound sensitivity when she wrote: "There are some for whom illness is made more difficult than it need be. Boswell shivers on the chilly boat journey from Greenwich to London, 'for the night air was so cold that it made me shiver. I was the more sensible of it from having sat up all the night before, recollecting and writing in my journal what I thought worthy of preservation' (of the sayings and doings of his friend). But Johnson, who 'was not in the least affected by the cold, scolded me as if my shivering had been a paltry effeminacy.' Another unfortunate is rebuked for a headache: 'At your age, sir, I had no head-ache.' There is one simple way to achieve serenity when (if ever) we meet Dr. Samuel Johnson: It is to be glad that he had never known 'shivering' or 'head-ache.' And also to remember that he is probably like a Spanish chestnut, rather prickly outside, but inside very good."[8]

In commenting on the health of a fellow Indian nurse, Kohila, Amy Carmichael said intuitively: "But, 'God help us if we are not better than our bodies' inclinations; the spirit of man will sustain his infirmity, is a great word for the ill, if only by the grace of the Lord, the Conqueror of pain, they can lay hold upon it. And Kohila did. Her fellow-nurses say of her, 'She was not an ordinary patient. She never forgot that she was a nurse, and so must be a perfect patient.' From time to time also there were the trials and tests that must be if life is to be more than a painted pretence. Each one of these had a share in shaping the child of this story. We thought of everything as a preparation for service, witness-bearing and soul-winning in the Place of Healing and in the villages. But now we know that it was preparation for another Service, Elsewhere."[9]

Joy in the Middle of Suffering

Perhaps some of Amy Carmichael's best words on illness, however, come from her book, *Rose from Brier*, where she wrote, "From the ill to the ill." Sensitive to a lack of understanding from those who are well, she wrote from the experience of her own illness.

"One day, after weeks of nights when, in spite of all that was done to induce sleep, it refused to come, except in brief distracted snatches, the mail brought a letter which discoursed with what sounded almost like pleasure on this 'enforced rest,' and the silly phrase rankled like a thorn. I was far too tired to laugh it off as one can laugh off things when one is well. So this was supposed to be rest? And was the Father breaking, crushing, 'forcing,' by weight of sheer physical misery, a child who only longed to obey his lightest wish? This word had what I now know was an absurd power to distress. It held such an unkind, such a false conception of our Father. Till that hour, although I was puzzled, I had not had one unhappy minute. I had been given peace in acceptance. The spirit can live above the flesh, and mine, helped by the tender love of our Lord Jesus and the dearness of all around me, had done so.

"But in that hour it was different, and I had no peace till I had heard deep within me soft and soothing words such as a mother uses: 'Let not your heart be troubled; do I not understand? What do such words matter to me or to thee?' And I knew that the Father understood his child, and the child her Father, and all was peace again."[10]

Approval from God is sometimes most intensely enjoyed when the suffering and the abrasiveness are hidden from man and known only to God. For the world is quick to laud those whom they can see as brave. A man with a cane or a child in braces is praised for bravery, and should be. But the person with depressive feelings or the person quietly suffering from the news of terminal illness in the life of a loved one is told to "rejoice" or "cheer up." The result in the sufferer is discouragement and, at times, a feeling that not even God understands.

We Christians are often too prone to associate suffering with a righteous consequence of sin, a sort of punishment or retribution from God. God does discipline his own, and sometimes there are painful consequences from sin. But often God chooses only his most valued children to entrust with the most painful of trials. Job is the most obvious biblical example of this kind of suffering. God could trust Job to believe in him when all earthly evidence for that belief seemed removed. Amy Carmichael once wrote:

"Trials are not 'chastisement.' No earthly father goes on chastising a loving child. That is a common thought about suffering, but I am quite sure that it is a wrong thought. Paul's sufferings were not that, nor are yours. They are battle wounds. They are signs of high confidence—honors. The Father holds his children very close to His heart when they are going through such rough places as this.

"'Thy *care* hath preserved my spirit'—a lovely Revised Version margin which helped me a few days ago—is my word for you (Job 10:12). Think of it; all day long you are being cared for, you are *in* His care.'"[11]

In an era of "Praise the Lord" theology, the real meaning of words like praise and joy may become lost to superficiality. For it is only in deep suffering that people know the depths of all emotion, whether it be pain that is almost unbearable even for one moment more, or joy that sweeps over the soul once that pain is gone. On an even more profound level, joy can exist *with* pain if one accurately defines that joy.

"Thunder-clouds are nothing to the Spirit of Joy. The only special reference to the joy of the Holy Spirit is bound up with the words 'much affliction,' much pressure. It is the rose under thunder-cloud again." Miss Carmichael included the words of Webb-Peploe as she continued."

" 'Joy is not gush; joy is not jolliness. Joy is simply perfect acquiescence in God's will, because the soul delights itself in God Himself. Christ took God as His God and Father, and that brought Him at last to say, "I delight to do thy will," though the cup was the cross, in such agony as no man knew. It cost Him blood. *It cost Him blood.* O take the Fatherhood of God in the blessed Son the Saviour, and by the Holy Ghost rejoice, rejoice in the will of God, and in nothing else. Bow down your heads and your hearts before God, and let the will, the blessed will of God, be done.'

"These weighty words were spoken by Prebendary Webb-Peploe to a gathering of Christians many years ago. In the silence that closed the hour, the speaker—some knew it—was laying, not for the first time, his Isaac on the altar of his God. It is the life lived that gives force to the words spoken. These words were not wind and froth. They sound through the years like the deep notes of a bell: *Joy is not gush; joy is not jolliness. Joy is perfect acquiescence in the will of God.*'

"This, then, is the call to the climbing soul. Expose yourself to the circumstances of his choice, for that is perfect acquiescence in the will of God. We are called to the fellowship of a gallant company, 'Ye become followers of us, and of the Lord,' wrote St. Paul to the men of Thessalonica. Who follows in their train?

> "Make me Thy mountaineer;
> I would not linger on the lower slope.
> Fill me afresh with hope, O God of hope,
> That undefeated I may climb the hill
> As seeing Him who is invisible,
>
> "Whom having not seen I love.
> O my Redeemer, when this little while
> Lies far behind me and the last defile

Is all alight, and in that light I see
My Saviour and my Lord, what will it be...?"[12]

When Others Fail Us

There is a buoyancy in helping others, a joy in seeing the positive results
of our help in the accomplishment of others. But each of us who in some
way ministers to the needs of people becomes at times drained, "weary in
well doing," disappointed over disappointing results. This brings upon us the
pain which combines fatigue with disappointment. Referring to Demas—a
biblical example of one who was led to Christ, trusted by Paul, and then
who turned back—Amy Carmichael explained this pain in disappointment:

> "After long prayer and toil, a soul has been led to Christ. By a thousand little
> signs you know that the miracle is happening for which you have waited so
> long. Then other influences begin to play upon that soul. Some Demas,
> once trusted and beloved, snatches at the chance to wound his forsaken
> Lord, and injects poison. The one who lately ran so well falters, looks back,
> goes back.

> "Then comes a terrific temptation to regard that Demas with eyes which see
> only his Demas qualities. And, as imperceptibly as water oozes through an
> earthen vessel, power to expect his return to peace and purity begins to
> pass. When the next new inquirer comes there may be a fear to meet him
> with buoyant, loving hope.

> "But this is fatal. Better be disappointed a thousand times—yes, and
> deceived—than once miss a chance to help a soul because of that faithless
> inhibition that grows, before we are aware of it, into suspicion and hard-
> ness. There is only one thing to be done. It is to realize that in us there is no
> good thing, nor faith, nor hope, nor even love; nothing human suffices here.
> All that we counted ours shrivels in the hot winds of disappointment: Thy
> servant hath not anything in the house. But the love of God suffices for any
> disappointment, for any defeat. And in that love is the energy of faith and
> the very sap of hope."[13]

When I feel that I have nothing left to give I find it helpful to realize that
"nothing human suffices here." It is then time for me to turn to him who will
always fill an empty surrendered vessel with himself. Sometimes when I
have nothing left to give, God is trying to tell me to slow down, to do less.

Speaking of the need to slow down and produce quality, Miss Carmichael
wrote: "We must learn, as the Tamil proverb says, to plough deep rather
than wide. Only God can plough both deep and wide." Then, quoting

Samuel Rutherford, " 'There is but a certain quantity of spiritual force in any man. Spread it over a broad surface, the stream is shallow and languid; narrow the channel and it becomes a driving force.'"[14]

Sometimes the person who disappoints us, however, is not someone we have only ministered to but someone who has ministered to us as well. He or she is our friend, not just part of our work, and in our tiredness and discouragement we need them. Then the pain has perhaps an even greater sting.

Of this Miss Carmichael said: "A beautiful quatrain is about silence where a disappointing friend is concerned; when those to whom we clung disappoint, keep the sad secret hid, cling to them still. The growing grain has husks; the water has its form; flowers have a scentless outer sheath of leaves."[15]

She continued: "Be careful also of your after-thinking as well as of your after-talking about any who have misjudged you. 'The hill-man thinks upon the beauty of his hills; the farmer thinks upon his fields that have yielded him rich crops; the good think on the boons bestowed by worthy men; the base man's thoughts are fixed on the abuse he has received,' is another old Tamil saying. Do not feed unloving thoughts. Remember His word, 'I forgave thee all that debt.'"[16]

And so Miss Carmichael concluded her discussion on friends with these marvelous words: "Why should we ever be bound? Of what account is anything if our King knows?"[17] Using Christ as our example is a great comfort in times of trial.

Overcoming Loneliness

We live in an age of loneliness which is symbolized by a desperate clinging to the past, escaping in alcohol and drugs, and involving ourselves in unlimited numbers of group activities, created not so much out of interest in a common theme as out of a desire to meet people—all to avoid loneliness.

Amy Carmichael found an ability to cope with loneliness as she looked at Christ's life; then she applied those principles which she had found in him to her own life, as she struggled with health problems and loneliness in India:

"Years later, in an hour of need, the Everlasting Comforter came through the Septuagint version of Psalm 150:18. His soul (Joseph's) entered into iron. It was not that others put him in irons (though they did, they hurt his feet with fetters), it was that he himself acquiesced in, willingly walked into the unexplained trial of his God's dealings with him. 'His soul entered, whole and entire in its resolve to obey God, into the cruel torture,' is Kay's note on that great matter. But what fathomless depths it must have held for our Lord Jesus when He set His face stedfastly to go to Jerusalem, Gethsemane, Calvary; and certain it is that whatever way of pain may open before any one of us, we find as we walk in it the marks of our dear Lord's footsteps leading on. He walked alone on that road so that we need never walk alone. No star, no flower, no song was Thine, but darkness three hours long.

"He was hard on Himself, but there is no hardness in His ways with us, and the dimmest pages in our story shine as we look back on them. We saw this once in parable. Some of us had gone to the coast to try to get rid of a persistent fever, and one night we bathed deliciously in a little bay between dark rocks. The night was moonless and starless, and the sea, except where it broke in ripples or waves, was as dark as sea can ever be. But when we came out of that water we were covered from head to foot in phosphorescent light, and when we sat down on the wet sand and dug our hands into it, diamonds ran between our fingers.

"There are lights that watch on occasion to appear. Such are the lights of strong consolation that have come when all was dark, whether because of some black trouble like the black seas of sin, or because of threatened harm or loss to that which is so much dearer to us than ourselves. For truly the love of the Lord whose brightness is as the light, who is Himself light, passeth all things for illumination, and if I say, Surely the darkness shall cover me; even the night shall be light about me."[18]

When the Trials Come Back Again

Much has been written about trial in the Christian life. Simplistically we assume that we suffer, recover and go on. We assume that the trials are gone forever. To the contrary often I find that trials reoccur. Just when I have thought I was finished with illness, or the hurt of death, or some other painful experience, it suddenly reappears.

In a chapter in *Gold By Moonlight*, entitled "And Then the Dark Wood Again," Miss Carmichael said of this "second wood," this repetition of trial:

"Perhaps this second wood may find the traveller startled or depressed by a recurrence of some trial which he had thought was well behind him. 'I have not passed this way heretofore,' he had said to himself when he entered the first dark wood. 'I shall henceforth return no more that way.' Nor does he, but perhaps just after a clear vision of peace from some House Beautiful he finds confronting him something very like the dark wood of earlier days. It is in fact a further reach of that wood.

"Here is one, perhaps an athlete, who has never been ill and never contemplated illness. He has become the vassal of Eternal *Love*. *Look, love, and
follow*: Prince Charlie engraved this motto on his seal when he came to call
the clans to suffer and die for him. The words are engraved upon the life of
this soldier who has looked, loved, and followed his Prince overseas. But his
first year sees him handicapped by illness. He recovers, is struck down
again, he who never was ill before. This repeated illness, battle-wound
though it be, so unexpected, so exhausting, can appear like a very dark
wood. Battle-wounds may sound heroic, but they do not feel so."[19]

Then as she continues in that same chapter: "The call to enter for the second
time into any painful experience is a sign of our Lord's confidence. It offers
a great opportunity. 'The most powerful thing in your life is your opportunity,' said Kleobulos of Lindos; it is also the most irretrievable. We must have
clearness of vision and courage and a quiet mind if we are to see it, and lay
hands upon it as it hurries past us on very quiet feet and disappears as utterly as the day that has gone: 'As thy servant was busy here and there' it was
gone. God give us vision and courage and a quiet mind."[20]

Purpose? It lies in those words: "The call to enter for the second time
into any painful experience is a sign of our Lord's confidence." To be
included as such a valued servant of our Lord is to be living in the perspective of eternity's values. It is to have purpose, to transcend mere coping.

Sometimes in a psychotherapist's office one sees symptoms come back
that had once gone. Trauma hits again just as one is recovering from previous trauma. Such occurrence may be interpreted by some as a sign of God's
disapproval. Rather, should we not see this reoccurring painful experience as
an indication of God's further opportunity for his child to trust the Lord
for the assurance and comfort he provides for traversing this second dark
wood? And what is true in the psychological realm is equally true in the
physical. For physical illness too may reoccur in the life of God's child.

Transcending Fears of Death

How often each of us must be reminded that the eternal value of a situation does not lie in our feelings or in what appears upon the surface. Death
is one of those experiences which we Christians feel we should not face
with fear or discomfort. Nevertheless, we can empathize with this expression
from one noted preacher who said, "I do not fear eternity but I do not look
forward to the process of dying."

An Indian nurse in the missionary compound where Miss Carmichael
worked was dying of cancer. Ponnammal was her name and she expressed

graphically the pain of dying as well as the realism of God's sustenance. Said Miss Carmichael of the experience:

> "'Last night,' [Ponnammal] said, 'I had less pain than usual, and my mind was clear. When the confusion passes, and the power to think returns, then my heart rises as if released from a weight; I can pray and praise. But first I examined myself to be sure all was well with me. For many days I had felt nothing, not even comfort, all was dimness and a blank and silence; then as I told my God about it he showed me that all through the days the joy of his salvation was within me, unchanged by any misery of pain. It was there, but I could not taste it. The darkness and the sadness of that time was caused by the medicine; *it was not that I had lost anything.* This comforted me, and I praised Him greatly and was content.' For many days her mouth had had that drawn look which those who have nursed anyone through sore suffering will know too well. But as she talked the old sweet, satisfied look returned, and all the old happy curves were there again. 'Oh, is it not wonderful!' she exclaimed with a sort of vigorous joyousness. 'For days and nights the waves beat hard on me, and then suddenly there is a great calm, and I lie back and rest.'
>
> "Then she asked for the last few verses of 1 Corinthians 15, repeating after me the words, 'Thanks be to God, which giveth us the victory.' And then I read the 46th Psalm to her, and she fell asleep."[21]

The experience was not one of the eradication of pain but rather one of triumph in the middle of pain because of God's provision. She did not annihilate pain and depression but she came through all of that darkness to a knowledge of God's approval.

Recovering From Fears of Failure

One form of suffering which Amy Carmichael pointed out and helped solve so realistically was the fear of failure. All of us conjure up giants in our lives—the "might-be's," the "what-if's." What if our child does not grow up to meet our hopes and expectations? What if our money doesn't last? What if our health gives way? What if I end up alone and helpless in my old age? Each of us has our own what-if's, and each of us may not entirely relate to the what-if's of our neighbor. Wrote Miss Carmichael:

"But we can be tormented by fear of failing before the end of a journey. We need not fear. It was George Tankervil, he who said,

'Though the day be never so long,
At last it ringeth to evensong,
Who out of weakness, was made strong.'

"He so greatly feared lest he should flinch from martyrdom, that to test himself he had a fire kindled in the chamber where he was confined, and sitting on a form before it, he put off his shoes and hose and stretched out his foot to the flame; but when it touched his foot, 'he quickly withdrew his leg, showing how the flesh did persuade him one way and the Spirit another way.' And yet a few hours later, when he came to the green place near the west end of St. Albans Abbey where the stake was set, he kneeled down, and when he had ended his prayer he arose with a joyful faith. Before they put the fire to him a certain knight went near and said softly, 'Good brother, be strong in Christ.' And he answered, 'I am so, I thank God.' So embracing the fire, he bathed himself in it, and calling on the name of the Lord, was quickly out of pain.

"Have we not often been like George Tankervil? We have imagined what was coming, and perhaps tested our constancy by some fire of our own kindling, and faith and courage have suddenly collapsed. For grace to endure and to conquer is never given till the moment of need, but when that moment comes? O Saviour, who dost not forget thy Calvary, hast thou ever failed the soul that trusted thee? Never, never. By the merits of thy Blood all is well, all shall be well."[22]

Amy Carmichael had her own what-if's. She feared that at the end of her life she would linger on to be a burden to others. Years before her death she had written in her journal: "Lord, teach me how to conquer pain to the uttermost henceforth, and grant this my earnest request. When my day's work is done, take me straight Home. Do not let me be ill and a burden or anxiety to anyone. O let me finish my course with joy and not with grief. Thou knowest there could be no joy if I knew I were tiring those whom I love best, or taking them from the children. Let me die of a battle-wound, O my Lord, not of a lingering illness."[23]

However, for years before she died, Miss Carmichael was totally bedridden. Here she triumphed in a deep way with God and some of her special insights in writing came during those years. During those last days she kept by her side the last stanza of an old hymn which epitomized her source of comfort:

"Green pastures are before me
Which yet I have not seen,
Bright skies will soon be o'er me
Where the dark clouds have been

My hope I cannot measure,
My path to life is free,
My Saviour has my treasure,
And He will walk with me."[24]

In all of her endeavors Christ was her motivation, her source of power, her lifetime goal. That made all the difference in her suffering.

The Constant Victory

It was a typically tropical day in a small coastal town in Mexico. I had come to rest, relax, write, yet I was still terribly tired. No book had been finished. Even my body had not responded to the rest as quickly as I had hoped. Feeling quite discouraged, but not wanting to impose that dreary feeling on my friends, I went off by myself for a while to be alone. I looked out at the ocean which was clear and blue, and felt nothing. Coconut palms and surrounding hills were green from the recent rains, but they too could not meet my need. I was irritated with the fatigue and the gloom of going home and facing once again a full schedule with not enough physical strength. Languidly I thumbed through the pages of one of my Amy Carmichael books. (I usually take one with me when I go on a trip.) My eyes fell on these words:

"For, lo, the winter is past, the rain is over and gone; the flowers appear on the earth; the time of the singing of birds is come...There has been a turning of the captivity and the hard weather has passed, but there is still something stark in our landscape...There is a fact, a memory, a possibility, that strikes up and faces us wherever we look. That knot of painful circumstances is there; that fear, that fearful thing, may be waiting in the shadows to spring upon us like a panther on a fawn."[25] Then in reference to a photograph full of the beauty of nature, yet also including a picture of an ancient ruin right in the middle of all the beauty, Miss Carmichael continues: "The picture is a figure of the true: it is full of grace and a lovely lightness, but it is the ruin that arrests the eye and gives character to the whole. Take it out, and you have merely a pretty page of scenery, and life is more than that. The charm of leaf and bud after a time of snow is not all that God has for those whom He is preparing to minister to others."[26]

My life, too, had its own "lovely lightness" but it had been the "knot of painful circumstances" which had intruded into my thinking even in this tropical paradise. I realized afresh that "life is more than that." The pain, the fatigue, the things I would like to erase from the landscape of my life are those very things which God was using to prepare me in my ministry for him. The challenge is that the ruin in my life, those painful things I would like to erase, not remain a mere ruin but be transformed by his hand into something positive.

God is in the process of bringing us to wholeness, to completeness, that we may be totally prepared for the fulfillment of his purposes in us. The process often includes fierce and fearful times. There may be ruins along the way. But we can be sure that in God's crucible we have the promise of a glorious, shining end. In Amy Carmichael's words:

"One day we took the children to see a goldsmith refine gold after the ancient manner of the East. He was sitting beside his little charcoal-fire. (He shall sit as a refiner: the gold or silversmith never leaves his crucible once it is on the fire.) In that red glow lay a common curved roof-tile; another tile covered it like a lid. This was the crucible. In it was the medicine made of salt, tamarind fruit and burnt brick-dust, and embedded in it was the gold. The medicine does its appointed work on the gold, 'then the fire eats it,' and the goldsmith lifts the gold out with a pair of tongs, lets it cool, rubs it between his fingers, and if not satisfied puts it back again in fresh medicine. This time he blows the fire hotter than it was before, and each time he puts the gold in the crucible the heat of the fire is increased. 'It could not bear it so hot at first, but it can bear it now; what would have destroyed it then helps it now.' 'How do you know when the gold is purified?' we asked him, and he answered, 'When I can see my face in it [the liquid gold in the crucible] then it is pure.'"[27]

Thus, when in us our Refiner sees his own image, he has indeed brought us to ultimate and true wholeness! To me this was a comforting insight. The ocean uplifted once more. The fatigue even seemed to lift a bit as I rejoined my friends. In the back of my mind I could not quite forget Amy Carmichael's poem which summarized all of my feelings at that moment— and indeed, what this book is really all about.

"Before the winds that blow do cease,
Teach me to dwell within Thy calm:
Before the pain has passed in peace,
Give me, my God, to sing a psalm.
Let me not lose the chance to prove
The fulness of enabling love,
O Love of God, do this for me:
Maintain a constant victory.

Before I leave the desert land
For meadows of immortal flowers,
Lead me where streams at Thy command
Flow by the borders of the hours,
That when the thirsty come, I may
Show them the fountains in the way.
O Love of God, do this for me:
Maintain a constant victory."[28]

Dwight L. Moody

Dwight L. Moody was born in Northfield, Massachusetts. He was a preacher and evangelist, and a close friend of men like F.B. Meyer and Charles H. Spurgeon. After Spurgeon's death, in token of their closeness, his wife sent Moody a Bible of Spurgeon's in which were inscribed the following words:

> "Mr. D.L. Moody, from Mrs. C.H. Spurgeon, in tender memory of the beloved one gone home to God. This Bible has been used by my precious husband, and is now given with unfeigned pleasure to one in whose hands its blessed service will be continued and extended."[1]

One of the most famous incidents of his life occurred when Moody attended a conference in Dublin and heard a man say: "The world has yet to see what

(1837–1899)

God can do with a thoroughly consecrated man." Moody responded: "God helping me, I will be that man." Dwight L. Moody was never again quite the same.

Moody himself once wrote a mini autobiography: "Some day you will read in the papers that D.L. Moody, of East Northfield, is dead. Don't you believe a word of it! At that moment I shall be more alive than I am now. I shall have gone up higher, that is all; gone out of this old clay tenement into a house that is immortal, a body that death cannot touch, that sin cannot taint, a body like unto His own glorious body. I was born of the flesh in 1837. I was born of the Spirit in 1855. That which is born of the flesh may die. That which is born of the Spirit will live forever."[2]

CHAPTER 6

Charles Spurgeon: Living with Depression

"I f I were a better Christian I wouldn't get so depressed" is a common statement from twentieth-century Christians when they feel discouraged or experience deep disappointment. Such an attitude may be fostered by some Christian literature that seems to equate depression with a lack of faith. Well-intentioned friends urge those who are depressed to "claim God's promises and be happy."

"God is the only tranquilizer I need," claimed one listener when she telephoned in on a TV talk show where I was a guest. This is by no means the first time I have heard this concept expressed. Apparently, "pray, and your problems will disappear" continues as a popular idea in some Christian circles. Perhaps some forget that we Christians are human. Forgiven, yes but still living within the boundaries of our humanity. We cannot be up, up, up all the time. A contrary view is neither scriptural nor tenable. Nobody can live on a continuing emotional high, for life comes inevitably equipped with valleys as well as mountaintops.

God does not promise that our faith will free us from all discouragement and conflict, but he does promise that the peace and power of his Spirit will give us the kind of joy that enables us to weather any afflictions of the body, mind and spirit. Amy Carmichael underscored this promise when she quoted H.W. Webb-Peploe's definition of Christian joy as that quiet, inner contentment that results from "perfect acquiescence in God's will."[1]

People in biblical times were certainly not always living on a spiritual high, nor did they attempt to use God as a giant tranquilizer to obliterate

their difficulties. Neither did they scoff at nor condemn as "unspiritual"
those who were hurting.

We in the twentieth century too often consider suffering to be synony-
mous with defeat. If it is such, then the "prince of preachers," a man who
lived with great depression and yet great joy in the Lord, must go down in
the annals of history as a man of enormous failure. So, too, must Jesus
Christ be judged for the "heaviness," the excruciating anguish of mind and
spirit he suffered by his perfect acquiescence in the will of God. To the contrary, within this total acquiescence in God's will is true joy and strength,
even when that will means a Gethsemane (see Matthew 26:36-39).

Joy With Pain

Today we can increase our ability to recover by learning from Charles
Spurgeon that times of depression cannot be eradicated, but that they can be
handled constructively.

"The strong are not always vigorous, the wise not always ready, the brave
not always courageous, and the joyous not always happy."[2] Such words
were not written in the twentieth century by a compromising pastor or psy-
chologist. They were spoken in the nineteenth century by that "prince of
preachers," Charles Haddon Spurgeon.

In dealing with something as common as money, Charles Spurgeon once
wrote, "During a very serious illness, I had an unaccountable fit of anxiety
about money matters. One of the brethren, after trying to comfort me, went
straight home, and came back to me bringing all the stocks and shares and
deeds and available funds he had, putting them down on the bed: 'There,
dear Pastor, I owe everything I have in the world to you, and you are quite
welcome to all I possess.' Of course I soon got better and returned it all to
my dear friend."[3] Such was the humanness of Spurgeon, for when it came to
money he was often plagued with the kind of anxiety to which many of us
can relate.

At the age of 19, he was called to the New Park Street Chapel, one of
the leading three (of the 113) Baptist churches of London. He was called
because an influential Baptist deacon said, "If you want to fill your empty
pews, send for a young man I heard in Cambridge by the name of Spurgeon."[4] Called he was, and the pews filled up until space became an increasing problem.

On October 19, 1856, crowds gathered in a new meeting place which
happened to be London's " 'largest, most commodious and most beautiful

nace, they might not rue the day afterwards in which they had been called to pass through the flame. There are none so tender as those who have been skinned themselves. Those who have been in the chamber of affliction know how to comfort those who are there. Do not believe that any man will become a physician unless he walks the hospitals; and I am sure that no one will become a divine, or become a comforter, unless he lies in the hospital as well as walks through it and has to suffer himself. God cannot make ministers—and I speak with reverence of His Holy Name—He cannot make a Barnabas except in the fire. It *is* there, and there alone, that He can make His sons of consolation; He may make His sons of thunder anywhere; but His sons of consolation He must make in the fire, and there alone. Who shall speak to those whose hearts have been broken also, and whose wounds have long run with the sore of grief? 'If need be,' then, 'ye are in heaviness through manifold temptations.'"[16]

Growth Through Distress

How easily we equate happiness with success and wellbeing. Even as Christians we often deceive ourselves into believing that we are obligated to achieve perpetual happiness. We even assume, at times, that because we are Christians happiness is owed to us as some kind of earned reward. The Bible does not teach such a principle; rather it promises a deep spiritual contentment which may exist even in the depth of suffering. Charles Spurgeon knew that spiritual growth and greatness are often mixed with pain: in his case, the pain of periodic and intense depression.

"Our work, when earnestly undertaken, lays us open to attacks in the direction of depression. Who can bear the weight of souls without sinking to the dust? Passionate longings after men's conversion, if not fully satisfied (and when are they?) consume the soul with anxiety and disappointment. To see the hopeful turn aside, the godly grow cold, professors abusing their privileges, and sinners waxing more bold in sin—are not these sights enough to crush us to the earth?...How can we be otherwise than sorrowful, while men believe not our report, and the divine arm is not revealed? All mental work tends to weary and to depress, for much study is a weariness of the flesh—but ours is more than mental work—it is heart work, the labour of our inmost soul...Such soul-travail as that of a faithful minister will bring on occasional seasons of exhaustion, when heart and flesh will fail. Moses' hands grew heavy in intercession, and Paul cried out, 'Who is sufficient for these things?' Even John the Baptist is thought to have had his fainting fits, and the apostles were once amazed, and were sore afraid."[17]

Rest Time is Not Waste

Sometimes depression can be cured or even avoided. Spurgeon could be very practical when speaking of recovery and prevention. As he stated earlier when giving the causes for depression, Spurgeon cited an unnecessary form of depression arising from too much study and too little exercise. As the author of more than 200 works and preacher of hundreds of sermons, such depression was a continuing problem for Spurgeon:" I confess that I frequently sit hour after hour praying and waiting for a subject, and that is the main part of my study. Almost every Sunday of my life I prepare enough outlines of sermons to last me for a month."[18]

Charles Haddon Spurgeon the most solemn place in the world was the pulpit. And he went into it week after week obviously depending upon the Holy Spirit. Such mental and spiritual intensity took its toll.

There can be little doubt that sedentary habits have a tendency to create despondency in some constitutions. "Burton, in his Anatomy of Melancholy, has a chapter upon this cause of sadness; and quoting from one of the myriad authors whom he lays under contribution, he says: 'Students are negligent of their bodies. Other men look to their tools: a painter will wash his pencils; a smith will look to his hammer, anvil, forge; a husbandman will mend his plough-irons, and grind his hatchet if it be dull; a falconer or huntsman will have an especial care of his hawks, hounds, horses, dogs, etc.; a musician will string and unstring his lute; only scholars neglect that instrument (their brain and spirits, I mean) which they daily use.'

"To sit long in one posture, poring over a book, or driving a quill, is in itself a taxing of nature; but add to this a badly ventilated chamber, a body which has long been without muscular exercise, and a heart burdened with many cares, and we have all the elements for preparing a seething cauldron of despair, especially in the dim months of fog—

> 'When a blanket wraps the day,
> When the rotten woodland drips,
> And the leaf is stamped in clay.'

"Let a man be naturally as blithe as a bird, he will hardly be able to bear up year after year against such a suicidal process; he will make his study a prison and his books the warders of a gaol, while nature lies outside his window calling him to health and beckoning him to joy. He who forgets the humming of the bees among the heather, the cooing of the wood pigeons in the forest, the song of birds in the woods, the rippling of rills among the rushes, and the sighing of the wind among the pines, need not wonder if his heart forgets to sing and his soul grows heavy. A day's breathing of fresh air upon the hills, or a few hours' ramble in the beechwood's umbrageous calm, would sweep the cobwebs out of the brain of scores of our toiling ministers who are now but half alive. A mouthful of sea air, or a stiff walk in the wind's face, would not give grace to the soul, but it would yield oxygen to the body, which is the next best.

> 'Heaviest the heart is in a heavy air,
> Ev'ry wind that rises blows away despair.'

"'The ferns and the rabbits, the streams and the trout, the fir trees and the squirrels, the primroses and the violets, the farmyard, the new-mown hay, and the fragrant hops—these are the best medicines for hypochondriacs, the surest tonics for the declining, the best refreshments for the weary.' For lack of opportunity, or inclination, these great remedies are neglected, and the student becomes a self-immolated victim."[19]

Much of our fatigue and depression is the result of refusal to take small breaks and short vacations. One weekend recently I escaped from the demands of patients to my favorite ocean cottage which has no telephones. I walked on the wet sand and thought about God's timelessness as I watched the waves crash against the rocks. By Monday I was refreshed and ready to go back to work because I had taken time away. Never should we underestimate the value of even small breaks.

Ahead of his time, Spurgeon was sensitive to the needs of the body as they relate to the needs of the mind. He had discovered the value of rest and recreation in averting and ameliorating depression.

Referring to Jesus' response to His weary disciples—"Let us go into the desert and rest awhile" (Mark 6:31)—Spurgeon commented:

"What? When the people are fainting? When they are like sheep without a shepherd? How can Jesus talk of rest? When the scribes and Pharisees, like wolves, are rending the flock, how can He take His followers on an excursion into a quiet resting place?...The Lord Jesus knows better. He will not exhaust the strength of His servants prematurely and quench the light of Israel. Rest time is not waste. It is economy to gather fresh strength. Look at the mower in the summer's day, with so much to cut down ere the sun sets. He pauses in his labour—is he a sluggard? He looks for his stone, and begins to draw it up and down his scythe, with rink-a-tink, rink-a-tink. Is that idle music—is he wasting precious moments? How much might he have mowed while he has been ringing out those notes on his scythe! But he is sharpening his tool, and he will do far more when once again he gives his strength to those sweeps which lay the grass prostrate in rows before him. Nor can the fisherman be always fishing; he must mend his nets. So even our vacation can be one of the duties laid upon us by the kingdom of God."[20]

In our work-oriented society, some of us are geared to feeling a sense of guilt regarding rest and recreation. Though we appear to place a premium on leisure time, many of us are prone to combining vacations with business trips or spending days off worrying about business or financial problems. In light of this, Spurgeon's point is profoundly significant: a vacation is a duty God requires of us!

Flawed Vessels

It is impossible to speak of depression as a problem arising only from one source. As each of us is a composite of body, mind and soul, problems in any of these areas of our personhood can cause depression. I sometimes deal with patients who have emotional problems arising from physical causes. These patients tend to have difficulty believing that their emotional negativism and hopelessness can be the result of physical malfunctions.

Spurgeon was far ahead of his time in perceiving this important relationship between emotions and the body. Perhaps this was due in part to his own deep suffering labeled as gout, which is now known to be a painful form of arthritis arising from an overabundance of uric acid in the system. In his physical weakness and pain he often slumped into the depths of despair. For that reason Spurgeon knew better than most people today the relationship between his emotions and his body:

> "Most of us are in some way or other unsound physically. 'Here and there we meet with an old man who could not remember that ever he was laid aside for a day; but the great mass of us labour under some form or other of infirmity, either in body or mind...As to mental maladies, is any man altogether sane? Are we not all a little off the balance? Some minds appear to have a gloomy tinge essential to their very individuality; of them it may be said, 'Melancholy marked them for her own'—fine minds withal, and ruled by noblest principles, but yet most prone to forget the silver lining, and to remember only the cloud...These infirmities may be no detriment to a man's career of special usefulness; they may even have been imposed upon him by divine wisdom as necessary qualifications for his peculiar course of service. Some plants owe their medicinal qualities to the marsh in which

they grow; others to the shades in which alone they flourish. There are precious fruits put forth by the moon as well as by the sun. Boats need ballast as well as sail; a drag on the carriage wheel is no hindrance when the road runs downhill. Pain has, probably, in some cases developed genius, hunting out the soul which otherwise might have slept like a lion in its den. Had it not been for the broken wing, some might have lost themselves in the clouds, some even of these choice doves who now bear the olive branch in their mouths and show the way to the ark. But where in body and mind there are predisposing causes to lowness of spirit it is no marvel if in dark moments the heart succumbs to them; the wonder in many cases is—and if inner lives could be written, men would see it so—how some...keep at their work at all, and still wear a smile upon their countenances...'Blessed are they that mourn,' said the Man of Sorrows, and let none account themselves otherwise when their tears are salted with grace. 'We have the treasure of the gospel in earthen vessels, and if there be a flaw in the vessel here and there, let none wonder.'"21

Compassion from Suffering

Many patients tell me how they have been able to help others. Sometimes the very best antidote for depression is the understanding another person can offer. Spurgeon through his own pain discussed compassion as an outgrowth of depression.

"How low the spirits of good and brave men will sometimes sink. Under the influence of certain disorders everything will wear a sombre aspect, and the heart will dive into the profundest days of misery. It is all very very well for those who are in robust health and full of spirits to blame those whose lives are [covered over] with melancholy, but the [pain] is as real as a gaping wound, and all the more hard to bear because it lies so much in the region of the soul that to the inexperienced it appears to be a mere matter of fancy and imagination. Reader, never ridicule the nervous and hypochondriacal, their pain is real—it is not imaginary...The mind can descend far lower than the body...flesh can bear only a certain number of wounds and no more, but the soul can bleed in ten thousand ways and die over and over again each hour. It is grievous to the good man to see the Lord whom he loves laying him in the sepulchre of desponding...yet if faith could but be allowed to speak she would remind the depressed saint that it is better to fall into the hand of the Lord than into the hands of men, and moreover she would tell the despondent heart that God never placed Joseph in a pit without drawing him up again to fill a throne...Alas, when under deep depression the mind forgets all this and is only conscious of its unutterable misery...It is an unspeakable consolation that our Lord Jesus knows this experience, right well, having with the exception of the sin of it, felt it all and more than all in Gethsemane when he was exceedingly sorrowful even unto death."[22]

By sharing his pain, Spurgeon was able to help others. Even in the pulpit, to a large congregation he once said: "I would go into the deeps a hundred times to cheer a downcast spirit. It is good for me to have been afflicted, that I might know how to speak a word in season to one that is weary."[23]

That such was true in Spurgeon's life was shown in a letter he received after a severe down period: "Here is a specimen showing how Spurgeon was able to comfort others with the same comfort whereby he was comforted. From Montreal came this rewarding letter.

> "'Oh, Mr. Spurgeon, that little word of yours, "I am feeling low," struck a chord which still vibrates in my spirit. It was to me like reading the Forty-second Psalm. I imagine there is nothing in your ministry to the saints that comes home more tenderly to tried and stricken souls than just what you there express, "I am feeling low." The great preacher, the author of The Treasury of David, this man sometimes, aye, often, "feels low" just as they do. In all their affliction he was afflicted—this is what draws hearts to Jesus; and the principle is just the same when the friends and intimates of Jesus "feel low." The fellow feeling, thus begotten, makes many wondrous kind.
>   Your friend in Jesus,
>   John Louson.'"[24]

Christians may find themselves vulnerable to criticism from Christians and non-Christians alike when they are suffering times of depression. Charles Spurgeon was certainly no exception. He was often criticized for his vulnerability to depression. But without the compassion Spurgeon demonstrated in his own affliction, countless others suffering like him would not have been comforted.

Renewal Through Prayer

Rather than withering under the pressure of depression or groveling in guilt over his supposed weakness or sin, Spurgeon proclaimed the relationship of anguish and prayer: "When our prayers are lowly...by reason of our despondency," Spurgeon wrote, "the Lord will bow down to them, the infinitely exalted Jehovah will have respect unto them. Faith, when she has the loftiest name of God on her tongue...dares to ask from Him the most tender and condescending acts of love. Great as He is, He loves His children to be bold with Him. Our distress is a forcible reason for our being heard by the Lord God, merciful, and gracious, for misery is ever the master argument with mercy."[25]

God never fails to hear our prayers. Indeed, the God who "numbers the hairs on our heads" and "preserves our tears in bottles" cannot fail to be concerned with our pain. But because He hears our prayers does not mean that He always gives us what we want, when we want it.

Again Spurgeon emphasized the importance of prayer as a weapon against depression in his famous work written about the Psalms. Quoting from Psalm 102:23,24—"He weakened my strength in the way; he shortened my days. I said, O my God, take me not away in the midst of my days"—Spurgeon said, in relationship to the psalmist's feelings and ultimate prayer: the psalmist "pours out his personal complaint. His sorrow had cast down his spirit, and even caused weakness in his bodily frame— and [he] was ready to lie down and die…He [gave] himself to prayer. What better remedy is there for depression? Good men should not dread death, but they are not forbidden to love life: for many reasons the man who has the best hope of heaven, may nevertheless think it desirable to continue here a little longer, for the sake of his family, his work, the church of God and even the glory of God itself. [They say,] do not swirl me away like Elijah in a chariot of fire, for as yet I have only seen half my days, and that a sorrowful half; give me to live till the flustering morning shall have softened into a bright afternoon of happier existence."[26]

We Shall Be Like Him

Too often we forget that Jesus Christ is God who became man and was subject to all the emotions that normal men feel. In a sermon preached at the Music Hall in Royal Surrey Gardens on November 7, 1858, Spurgeon drew upon the reality of Jesus the man, and uniquely presented depression as "being in heaviness" as our Lord was at times in his earthly life:

> "It is a rule of the kingdom that all members must be like the head. They are to be like the head in that day when He shall appear. 'We shall be like Him, for we shall see Him as He is.' But we must be like the head also in His humiliation, or else we cannot be like Him in His glory. Now you will observe that our Lord and Saviour Jesus Christ very often passed through much of trouble, without any heaviness. When He said, 'Foxes have holes, and the birds of the air have nests, but the Son of Man hath not where to lay His head,' I observe no heaviness. I do not think He sighed over that. And

when athirst He sat upon the well, and said, 'Give me to drink,' there was no heaviness in all His thirst. I believe that through the first years of His ministry, although He might have suffered some heaviness, He usually passed over His troubles like a ship floating over the waves of the sea. But you will remember that at last the waves of swelling grief came into the vessel; at last the Saviour Himself, though full of patience, was obliged to say, 'My soul is exceeding sorrowful, even unto death'; and one of the evangelists tells us that the Saviour 'began to be very heavy.' What means that, but that His spirits began to sink? There is more terrible meaning yet...the surface meaning of it is that all His spirits sank with Him. He had no longer His wonted courage, and though He had strength to say, 'Nevertheless, not my will, but thine be done,' still the weakness did not prevail, when He said, 'If it be possible let this cup pass from me.' The Saviour passed through the brook, but He 'drank of the brook by the way'; and we who pass through the brook of suffering must drink of it too. He had to bear the burden, not with His shoulders omnipotent, but with shoulders that were bending to the earth beneath a load. And you and I must not always expect a giant faith that can remove mountains. Sometimes even to us the grasshopper must be a burden, that we may in all things be like our head."[27]

In truth, the black clouds of depression never permanently left Spurgeon's life until he entered into life with his Savior. Yet, through all those earthly days, God was enough, "the true source of all consolation."

Referring to Psalms 102:3 where the psalmist says, "For my days are consumed like smoke," Spurgeon commented: "My grief has made life unsubstantial to me. I seem to be but a puff, a vapour which has nothing in it, and is soon dissipated. The metaphor is very admirably chosen, for, to the unhappy, life seems not merely to be frail, but to be surrounded by so much that is darkening, defiling, blinding, and depressing, that, sitting down in despair, they compare themselves to men wandering in a dense fog . . ." Spurgeon continued: "Now the writer's mind is turned away from his personal and relative troubles to the true source of all consolation, namely, the Lord himself, and his gracious purposes toward his own people. 'But thou, O Lord, shalt endure forever.' I perish, but thou wilt not."[28]

The Light Beyond

In spite of, and very likely because of, the depression in Spurgeon's life, he became a spiritual giant for God. Biographer Richard Day confesses that "he was unexpectedly moved to tears in reading one of Spurgeon's travelog lectures." Within seven lines of the end, Spurgeon suddenly concluded his remarks: "If you cannot travel, remember that our Lord Jesus Christ is more glorious than all else that you could ever see. Get a view of Christ and you have seen more than mountains and cascades and valleys and seas can ever show you. Earth may give its beauty, and stars their brightness, but all these put together can never rival Him."29

"Tirshatha"—as Susannah Spurgeon called her husband, using the Hebrew word for the Reverence—spent some of his winter months in Mentone, France, because his body could not endure the chill of London. Susannah, who became an invalid at the age of 33, was unable to travel and go with him. During one of those winter separations, Spurgeon wrote this to his wife: "You are the precise form in which God would make a woman for such a man as I." Such a woman she truly was. Many times Spurgeon came home from meetings at the great tabernacle exhausted and in the grip of depression. Then she would read to him from Baxter's *Reformed Pastor*—'he would weep at my feet, and I would weep too.'"30

Susannah herself knew the purposes of suffering. Watching a crackling oak log on the fireplace one evening, she wrote: "We are like this old log. We should give forth no melodious sounds were it not for the fire."31.

In God's gracious plan, Susannah Spurgeon was strong enough to go to France with her husband the year of his death. "When he lay dying in Mentone, Susannah lingered beside him. She wept softly as he lay for hours unconscious. She smiled bravely through her tears when for short intervals he spoke with her. Out of her grief she wrote: 'Perhaps of greatest price among the precious things which this little book (the *Secret Diary*) reveals, is the beloved author's personal and intense love for the Lord Jesus. He lived in his embrace; like the apostle John, his head leaned on Jesus' bosom ('Jesu' was his private and intimate term of endearment for his Lord). The endearing terms, used in the Diary and never discontinued, were not empty words.'

"When the end drew near, he whispered, 'Susie.' She bent close to listen, clasped his hand in hers and said, 'Yes, dear Tirshatha.' And he murmured—the last words before he saw him face to face—'Oh, wifie, I have had such a blessed time with my Lord.'"32

"Years before [Spurgeon] had spoken of death: 'The dying saint is not in a flurry; he keeps to his old pace—he walks. The last days of a Christian are the most peaceful of his whole career; many a saint has reaped more joy and knowledge when he came to die than ever he knew while he lived. When there is a shadow, there must be a light somewhere. The light of Jesus shining upon death throws a shadow across our path; let us therefore rejoice for the Light beyond!'"33

Brother Lawrence

He was a lay brother of the Carmelita Order. In spite of a natural aversion to work in the kitchen, Brother Lawrence quoted the poem:

> "'Lord of all pots and things...
> Make me a saint by getting meals
> And washing up the plates!'

> "...and he could say, 'The time of business does not with me differ from the time of prayer; and in the noise and clatter of my kitchen, while several persons are at the same time calling for different things, I possess God in as great tranquillity as if I were upon my knees at the blessed sacrament.'

"Except for the kitchen, we know little of his career: only that he was born Nicholas Herman in French Lorraine, that he was lowly and unlearned in the teaching of the schools, that he served briefly as footman and soldier, and under the whips of God and conscience was driven to become a Lay brother

100

(Nicholas Herman)

among the barefooted Carmelites at Paris in the year 1666 and was known forever after that as 'Brother Lawrence.' His conversion, at eighteen, was the result of the mere sight on a midwinter day of a dry and leafless tree standing gaunt against the snow; it stirred deep thoughts within him of the change the coming spring would bring. From that moment on he grew and waxed strong in the knowledge and love and favor of God, endeavoring constantly, as he put it, 'to walk as in His presence.' No wilderness wanderings, no bitter winter seasons of soul or spirit, seem to have intervened between the Red Sea and the Jordan of his experience. A wholly consecrated man, he lived his life as though he were a singing pilgrim on the march, as happy in serving his fellow monks and brothers from the monastery kitchen as in serving God in the vigil of prayer and penance. He died at eighty years of age, full of love and years and honored by all who knew him, leaving a name which has been 'as precious ointment poured forth.'"[1]

"They also serve who only stand and waite." (John Milton - 1655)

CHAPTER 7

Hudson Taylor: Drawing on God's Provision

It was late spring a number of years ago. The weather was beginning to warm up and once again I began my frequent visits to the ocean. This year it was different, however. I had just started a new career. I was building a private counseling practice, after teaching school for 12 years. Until that practice expanded I had plenty of time to go to the beach—and to think. I kept remembering that I had given up a fixed income, paid sick leave and vacations, and general security in exchange for the unknown. Unknown, that is, except that God had led me; so the way was known at least to him.

It was sunset as I drove home from the beach on a street overlooking the sea and shaded by large trees. Waves of doubt caused me to feel restless and a little frantic. How would I live until I had time to build up the practice? What if I didn't make it financially? Then, with as much reality as that deepening sunset, there flashed across my mind the thoughts of a passage in Scripture:

"Ye cannot be in service unto God and unto riches. For this cause I say unto you: Be not anxious for your life what ye shall eat or what ye shall drink, or for your body what ye shall put on: Is not the life more than food? And the body more than raiment? Observe intently the birds of the heaven, that they neither sow nor reap nor gather into barns, and yet your heavenly Father feedeth them: Are not ye much better than they?

"But who from among you, being anxious can add to his stature one cubit? And about clothing why are ye anxious? Consider well the lilies of the field how they grow,—They toil not neither do they spin; and yet I say unto you not even Solomon in all his glory was arrayed like one of these!

"Now if the grass of the field—which today is and tomorrow into an oven is cast—God thus adorneth how much rather you, little of faith?

"Do not then be anxious saying, What shall we eat? Or what shall we drink? Or wherewithal shall we be arrayed?

"For all these things the nations seek after,—For your heavenly Father knoweth that ye are needing all these things. But be seeking first the kingdom and its righteousness—And all these things shall be added unto you" (Matthew 6:24-33, *The Emphasized Bible*).

Deep within myself, I knew that God would provide for me in an undertaking which had been instigated at his prodding. Where there had been fear there was now peace and a sense of excitement over how and when God would work. That frame of mind does not come to me easily, so I knew that it had surely come from God.

Similarly, a few years ago I spent some time in a small primitive town in Mexico. It is a place of exquisite beauty and peace. It is also remote from modern medical help and therefore not the best place to become ill. One morning I woke up with what I knew was more than a simple case of Montezuma's Revenge. I was sick and feverish. Because I am severely allergic to many medications, I wanted to avoid any local cures.

As I lay in bed that afternoon I calmly asked God to heal me. A logical request since I firmly believed that God's purposes for my life were still alive and real and that they required health. The result was a shaky but increasing return to physical wellbeing by the evening.

I do not believe that God unfailingly answers our prayers for healing with an answer of "yes." Sometimes he says "no" or "wait." Or, he chooses to give partial help. But at a time when I was without usable medical attention God undertook to do the whole job himself, an experience that was very bolstering to my faith in future days. God had provided for my needs as my life was centered in his will. He had not prevented my illness nor did he eliminate illness on future trips. But he did provide for my physical needs. He healed when that was necessary. God is not in the business of eradicating our problems, but he is definitely the One who supplies our needs in the middle of those problems.

God's Supply for God's Work

Hudson Taylor, the man who almost single-handedly opened up the interior of China to Christianity, learned, first as a young preacher in England, a principle of God's provision: "God's work done in God's way will never lack God's supplies."[1] One might add to that: "God's person, bent on doing God's will, shall have God's supply."

To Hudson Taylor a significant beginning in this life of trusting God for all practical supply came late one evening: "After concluding my last service about ten o'clock that night, a poor man asked me to go and pray with his wife, saying that she was dying. I readily agreed, and on the way asked him why he had not sent for the priest, as his accent told me he was an Irishman. He had done so, he said, but the priest refused to come without a payment of eighteen pence, which the man did not possess as the family was starving. Immediately it occurred to my mind that all the money I had in the world was the solitary half-crown, and that was in one coin; moreover, that while the basin of water-gruel I usually took for supper was awaiting me and there was sufficient in the house for breakfast in the morning, I certainly had nothing for dinner on the coming day.

"Somehow or other there was at once a stoppage in the flow of joy in my heart. But instead of reproving myself I began to reprove the poor man, telling him that it was very wrong to have allowed matters to get into such a state as he described, and that he ought to have applied to the relieving officer. His answer was that he had done so, and was told to come at eleven o'clock the next morning, but that he feared his wife might not live through the night.

"'Ah,' thought I, 'if only I had two shillings and a sixpence instead of this half-crown, how gladly would I give these poor people a shilling!' But to part with the half-crown was far from my thoughts. I little dreamed that the truth of the matter simply was that I could trust God plus *one-and-sixpence,* but was not prepared to trust Him only, without any money at all in my pocket.

"My conductor led me into a court, down which I followed him with some degree of nervousness. I had found myself there before, and at my last visit had been roughly handled...Up a miserable flight of stairs into a wretched room he led me, and oh what a sight there presented itself! Four of five children stood about, their sunken cheeks and temples telling unmistakably the story of slow starvation, and lying on a wretched pallet was a poor, exhausted mother, with a tiny infant thirty-six hours old moaning rather than crying at her side.

"'Ah!' thought I, 'If I had two shillings and a sixpence, instead of half-a-crown, how gladly should they have one-and-sixpence of it.' But still a wretched unbelief prevented me from obeying the impulse to relieve their distress at the cost of all I possessed.

"It will scarcely seem strange that I was unable to say much to comfort these poor people. I needed comfort myself. I began to tell them, however, that they must not be cast down; that though their circumstances were very distressing there was a kind and loving Father in heaven. But something within me cried, 'You hypocrite! Telling these unconverted people about a kind and loving Father in heaven and not prepared yourself to trust him without a half-a-crown.'

"I nearly choked. How gladly would I have compromised with conscience, if I had had a florin and sixpence! I would have given the florin thankfully and kept the rest. But I was not yet prepared to trust in God alone, without the sixpence.

"To talk was impossible under these circumstances, yet strange to say, prayer was a delightful occupation in those days. Time thus spent never seemed wearisome and I knew no lack of words. I seemed to think that all I should have to do would be to kneel down and pray, and that relief would come to them and to myself together."[2]

Perhaps at this time in his life Taylor began to learn on a deep gut level that God does not usually work in such a simplistic way. He cooperates with us to work out the meeting of our needs rather than just eliminating those needs. And thus we grow and learn to trust God more.

In his process of learning this trust, Taylor continued:

"'You asked me to come and pray with your wife,' I said to the man; 'let us pray.' And I knelt down.

"But no sooner had I opened my lips with, 'Our Father who art in heaven,' than conscience said within, 'Dare you mock God? Dare you kneel down and call him "Father" with that halfcrown in your pocket?'

"Such a time of conflict then came upon me as I had never experienced before. How I got through that form of prayer I know not, and whether the words uttered were connected or disconnected. But I arose from my knees in great distress of mind. "The poor father turned to me and said, 'You see what a terrible state we are in, sir. If you can help us, for God's sake.'

"At that moment the word flashed into my mind, 'Give to him that asketh of thee.' And in the word of a King there is power.

"I put my hand into my pocket and slowly drawing out the half-crown gave it to the man, telling him that it might seem a small matter for me to relieve them, seeing that I was comparatively well off, but that in parting with that coin I was giving my all; but that what I had been trying to tell them was indeed true, God really was a Father and might be trusted. And how the joy came back in full tide to my heart! I could say anything and feel it then, and the hindrance to blessing was gone—gone, I trust, forever.

"Not only was the poor woman's life saved, but my life, as I fully realized, had been saved too. It might have been a wreck...had not grace at that time conquered and the striving of God's Spirit been obeyed.

"I well remember that night as I went home to my lodgings how my heart was as light as my pocket. The dark, deserted streets resounded with a hymn of praise that I could not restrain. When I took my basin of gruel before retiring, I would not have exchanged it for a prince's feast. Reminding the Lord as I knelt at my bedside of his own Word, 'He that giveth to the poor lendeth to the Lord,' I asked him not to let my loan be a long one, or I should have no dinner the next day. And with peace within and peace without, I spent a happy, restful night.

"Next morning my plate of porridge remained for breakfast, and before it was finished the postman's knock was heard at the door. I was not in the habit of receiving letters on Monday, as my parents and most of my friends refrained from posting on Saturday, so that I was somewhat surpnsed when the landlady came in holding a letter or packet in her wet hand covered by her apron. I looked at the letter, but could not make out the handwriting. It was either a strange hand or a feigned one, and the postmark was blurred. Where it came from I could not tell. On opening the envelope I found nothing written within, but inside a sheet of blank paper was folded a pair of kid gloves from which, as I opened them in astonishment, half-a-sovereign fell to the ground."[3]

Principles of God's Supply

God's work done in God's way had received God's supply. Need had not been eradicated, for there will always be great need on this earth. The need had been supplied, which is a basic principle of God's work.

In all fairness it should be added that Taylor lived in an economy different than ours. Additionally one must glean from great lives principles of living rather than strict dogma. For it is dangerous to become a carbon copy of anyone.

To illustrate, I know an elderly lady who gave all she possessed to a radio broadcast under the duress of questioning her loyalty to God unless she so gave. A few months later she was living in misery with the grudging help of some relatives.

Each one of us must consider his or her finances in the light of God's will for our individual lives—each with its own needs.

There is another principle of truth to be gleaned, however, from Taylor's experience with the coin. As he himself expressed it, "If we are faithful to God in little things, we shall gain experience and strength that will be helpful to us in the more serious trials of life." More than that, God's training is unique for each of us. Taylor's "more serious trials of life" later in China, forced him to the extreme of faith. The loss of his wife and children and loss of his missionary co-workers were all to weigh heavily upon this man. At these times he would pace his study for hours, calming himself as he softly sang,

> "Jesus, I am resting, resting,
>   In the joy of what Thou art;
> I am finding out the greatness
>   Of Thy loving heart."

Truly "the life that was to be exceptionally fruitful had to be rooted and grounded in God in no ordinary way."[4]

It was in experiences such as that of the coin that Hudson Taylor learned what George Muller had also learned: *God's work can be done expansively and with quality, and we can expect God's supply.* The needs would never go away. They would remain constant and daily. But they would unfailingly be met in God's way and in God's time.

God's Expansive Supply

In Taylor's founding of the China Inland Mission, perhaps one of the greatest foreign missions, Taylor brought together deeply dedicated Christians who gave and were given to. They gave up this world's goods. Yet years later, for example; when his daughter-in-law and biographer, Geraldine Taylor, was in need of rest in the middle of her writing, she was sent to a lovely ocean resort for six months—with household help! And she should have been.

Individual saints must consider their finances in the light of God's will for *their* life with *its* needs. Sometimes God asks for a plunge of faith financially. Then do it! Sometimes he asks for hard core common sense. Then use it! An older person lovingly cared for by five adult children *may* be more generous financially than one who has no living relative. Hudson Taylor in his youth could more reasonably give away his last coin than perhaps a Taylor facing open heart surgery for his child or the poverty of his parents. For it is a biblical principle that one should care for those of his own household first. Even apart from direct Christian teaching, this principle is considered valid in most people's thinking.

In commenting upon the absolute degradation and ruin of the Ik, a tribe in Uganda, and applying his conclusions to the Western world, anthropologist Colin Turnbull says: "The rot is in all of us, for how many of us would be willing to divide our riches among our own family, let alone the poor or needy, beyond, of course, what we can easily afford—for if we were willing, why have we not done it?"[5] Should those in the Body of Christ have lower standards?

On this principle Muller built orphanages which excelled all others in England at that time. For Muller believed that if God's work was to be done, it was to be done well. Reports of Muller's success greatly influenced the life of Hudson Taylor in China and that of Amy Carmichael in Dohnavur in her work with children rescued from the temples of South India. Taylor, Muller, and Carmichael held several of the same basic principles—with Muller as a major influence on the other two. Predominant was their conviction that God's work done in God's way would receive God's supply.

They believed a second principle: that one could move people by prayer alone, which meant that no pledges were signed, no financial pleas expressed. And certainly not least, they each believed that if they were in the employment of a King, the work could afford to have quality. Since Muller's success based on these principles was dramatic, was influential on the work of God throughout the world, and is pertinent to us today, a lengthy quotation of his work is appropriate in connection with our thoughts of God's provision.

A visitor to Muller's orphanage observed in detail the following:

"On entering the grounds in which two of the houses stand, we passed the lodge, a neat little cottage on the right, and proceeded along the pathway by the side of the carriage-drive, which, together with a well-trimmed lawn and some pretty flowerbeds, separates No. 1 House from No. 2. There are large pieces of ground surrounding each of the houses, devoted to the cultivation of vegetables. The perfect order and neatness characterizing everything outside the establishment gave us a good intimation of what we might expect within; nor were we disappointed.

"The Orphan House No. 1, which contains usually 140 girls above seven years of age, 80 boys of the same age, and 80 infants of either sex, was that we first visited; but in describing it we shall follow that order which seems best fitted to give a clear understanding of the establishment, and not that in which the different parts are—to save time—shown to visitors.

"There are three school-rooms—boys', girls'; and infants'—all large, airy, and cheerful-looking apartments. The girls, which is shown first of the three, is very spacious and lofty, situated on the ground-floor, and well fitted up with the best modern maps and other helps for learning. As our party, numbering some sixty or seventy, entered, we beheld about one hundred and twenty girls, sitting at work at low desks; all clothed alike in blue print frocks and neat pinafores, and with their hair cut short behind, but arranged with the greatest neatness. On a signal from the principal teacher, who was stationed on a small platform, with a desk in front, the girls all stood up and placed their hands behind them. At another signal one of the orphans struck up a cheerful song, which the rest at once joined in, and all marched out in single file, with as much precision in their steps as any of our modern volunteer corps would exhibit. The effect of this sight was really very striking; and he who can witness unmoved these helpless orphans winding their way between the desks, to the music of the touching songs which they sang, one after another, must indeed be made of very impenetrable materials. As they passed round the ends of the desks in front of the visitors, who lined the walls on either side, I looked carefully at the features of each child, and, although in some cases I saw evident traces of disease, inherited, doubtless, from the parents whom they had lost, still there was a general appearance of health and cheerfulness in their happy faces.

"Then we were taken to the girls' cloak and show room, where we found a vast number of serviceable plaid cloaks hanging up around the room, for winter wear. Each girl, too, has three pairs of shoes for use—a mark of sound economy on Mr. Muller's part, as every *paterfamilias* well knows." Continuing, the report provided more details which pointed out not only God's supply, but even more particularly the quality of that supply:

"The boys' school-room does not materially differ from that of the girls. There were, at our entrance, about 80 boys seated at desks, dressed all alike in blue cloth jackets and corduroy trousers. Their appearance was certainly that of vigorous health. They looked sturdy, good-tempered fellows. At the word of command they all rose from their seats, and marched one after another between the desks to the air of some spirited song, just as the girls had before. Two separate rooms are appropriated as work-rooms also—one for the boys, and one for the girls; the former are taught, a few at a time, to knit and mend their own stockings, and the girls to make their own garments, under the superintendence of a teacher who does the cutting out for them. Then come the play-rooms, one for boys and another for girls. These are large, lofty rooms, with a few low forms, and nothing else in the shape of furniture. These are, of course, only intended for use in bad weather, at least in the case of the boys. For there is a capital court for playing in for each class of orphans, and swings and other apparatus for exercise and play. The girls' playroom was provided with large cupboards, divided into small pigeon-holes, one for each child, well stored with dolls, dolls' houses, and a variety of other toys, the gifts, sometimes of relatives (who are allowed to visit the orphans once a month), sometimes of ladies, who present them to the teachers to be used as rewards.

"The infant department in the Orphan House never fails to arrest the attention of visitors. Would that we could adequately bring before the reader the "infant school," with its two hundred little ones, or nearly so—many not more than three years of age. "We must say a few words about the 'infant nursery.' Some infants, it should be remembered, are taken in so young that they are literally babies, and these are nursed in a small comfortable room by a motherly-looking head nurse, assisted by two or three of the elder girls. It was a touching sight to watch these helpless infants toddling about with pretty horses or dolls in their hands, and some in the arms of their nurses. Around the room, too, we noticed several little basket beds in which these tiny babies might be placed, when overcome with sleep, with all the fondness of a mother's love."

Again emphasizing the quality with which God's work can and must be done, the narrative continued:

"Many visitors seem to regard as one of the prettiest sights in the whole establishment the 'infants' wardrobe.' It was a room about twenty feet long, and ranged on each side of the room stood painted deal presses, divided into small pigeonholes, in each of which were laid by, neatly folded up, small duplicates of the various articles of clothing worn by the infants. The one side was set apart for the girls' wardrobes, each little pile of clothing being crowned by a pretty little straw bonnet, and each garment being most carefully and neatly rolled up and pinned together. On the opposite side stood the same number of presses for the boys' clothes, and on the top of each tiny wardrobe that occupied the pigeon-holes, there was placed a little blue cloth cap. It is a fact, that scarcely any part of the house affects strangers so much as this infants' wardrobe; and it is a common thing to see tears in the eyes of one and another of the visitors, as they gaze on the exquisite order and nicety which prevail on every side, and think of the tender love which had so wonderfully cared for the smallest wants of these helpless little ones.

"Next to the infants' wardrobe room comes the infants' dormitory. At the end of the dormitory is a passage on each side of which are situated the private rooms of the matrons and teachers. These were most comfortably furnished, and quite in keeping with the station of those who occupy such positions in the Orphan Houses. Each individual has a separate apartment.

"The infants' dormitory, to which we have referred, is a spacious room, with abundance of air and light—filled with little tiny bedsteads. These are all of iron, painted of a light yellow color, and many fitted round with railings to preserve the younger babes from falling out. The beds are ranged in three rows from one end of the room to the other. There is no other article of furniture in the room of any description. Four larger beds—two at each end of the room—are occupied by the elder girls who take charge of the forty little orphans who nightly sleep in this cheerful room. Forty other infant orphans occupy the corresponding room to this, which we were afterwards shown.

"There is a third bed-room for girls, in which 140 female orphans sleep—two girls occupying one bed. The same marvelous cleanliness of floors, and spotless purity of quilts and bedclothes, with which our party was so impressed in the infants' dormitory, strikes us here. One good woman, in the height of her amazement, exclaimed, looking at the well-scrubbed boards, "Why, you might eat your dinner off them!" Another visitor, of the opposite sex, whose face was an index to the benevolence which filled his heart, observed, as he gazed at the beds, with the bed-clothes folded down with the utmost nicety and precision: 'Ah, they would never have slept in such beds if their parents had lived!' Great indeed was the admiration which this comfortable apartment elicited from our party. But it is impossible to describe the effect with pen and ink; it must be seen to be understood. At the end of the room there is a small window, opening into a bed-room occupied by one of the teachers, who is thus enabled to overlook the movements of the children. We afterwards saw the dormitories for boys, which it is unnecessary to describe, as they correspond exactly with the one just mentioned, except that only forty children sleep in each. Besides these, there is a small dormitory with eight beds in it for the elder girls, usually called 'housegirls,' as they are engaged in house-work, and are on the point of being sent out to service. Each of these has the privilege of a good strong box to hold her clothes in. These girls daily assist the servants in the general work of the house.

"After we had seen the infants' wardrobes, we were invited to inspect two other wardrobe rooms. The first we came to was the boys'. The arrangement of this room exactly agreed with that containing the infants' clothes. Each boy has a square compartment, in which to keep his clothes, with his number marked, in one of the large deal presses that line the room. Six boys, we were told, are draughted out to take charge of the wardrobes, and see that everything is kept in proper order. When their term of service is expired, their place is supplied by six others, until each boy in the house, of a fit age, has taken his turn. The boys have each three suits of clothes. The girls' wardrobe room corresponded with that for the boys, except that it is much larger. There were the same lofty painted deal presses, subdivided into innumerable little pigeon-holes. The girls have five changes of dress. Three blue print frocks for ordinary wear in the house, a lilac pattern dress for Sundays during the summer months, and a brown merino dress for winter wear. The girls make and mend all their own clothes. Six girls in rotation take charge of all the female wardrobes of the house; just as in the case of the boys.

"The dining-room where all the orphans take their meals is a spacious apartment filled with long narrow tables and forms, all as white almost as the paper on which the reader's eye is now fixed. While we were inspecting this room, we noticed some of the elder girls employed in spreading the snow-white table-cloths for the evening meal. Others at the same time entered the room with trays loaded with bread-and-butter. Soon afterwards, some hundreds of cups filled with milk-and-water were placed upon the tables; but the orphans were not called to tea until after the visitors had left."[6]

God's work was done in God's way and did receive God's supply!

A Chain of Supply

There is an incident which shows the remarkable, God-given relationship between Taylor and Muller. A servant had made off with Mr. Taylor's belongings and proof was given. Wrote Geraldine Taylor:

"For the recovery of the property it would not have been difficult to institute legal proceedings, and Mr. Taylor was strongly urged to secure the punishment of the thief; but the more he thought about it the more he shrank from anything of the sort. Yoh-hsi was one whose salvation he had earnestly sought, and to hand him over to cruel, rapacious underlings who would only be too glad to throw him into prison that he might be squeezed of the last farthing would not have been in keeping, he felt, with the spirit of the Gospel. Finally concluding that his soul was worth more than the forty pounds worth of things he had stolen, Mr. Taylor decided to pursue a very different course.

"'So I have sent him a plain, faithful letter,' he wrote in the middle of August, 'to the effect that we know his guilt, and what its consequences might be to himself; that at first I had considered handing over the matter to the Ya-men, but remembering Christ's command to return good for evil I had not done so, and did not wish to injure a hair of his head.

"'I told him that he was the real loser, not I; that I freely forgave him, and besought him more earnestly than ever to flee from the wrath to come. I also added that though it was not likely he would give up such of my possessions as were serviceable to a Chinese, there were among them foreign books and papers that could be of no use to him but were valuable to me, and that those at least he ought to send back.

"'If only his conscience might be moved and his soul saved, how infinitely more important that would be than the recovery of all I have lost. Do pray for him.'

"In course of time, and far away in England, this letter came into hands for which it had never been intended. Mr. George Muller from Bristol, founder of the well-known Orphan Homes, read it with thankfulness to God, finding in the circumstances an exemplification of the teachings of the Lord himself. His sympathies were drawn out to the young missionary who had acted in what he felt to be a Christ-like spirit, and from that time Hudson Taylor had an interest in his prayers.

"But more than this. As soon as the incident became known to him, he sent straight out to China a sum sufficient to cover Mr. Taylor's loss, continuing thereafter to take a practical share in his work, until in a time of special need he was used of God as the principal channel of support to the China Inland Mission. And all this grew out of one little act, as it might seem, of loyalty to the Master at some personal cost. Only there are no little acts when it is a question of faithfulness to God. And it was just his simple adherence, in every detail, to scriptural principles that gradually inspired confidence in Hudson Taylor and his methods, and won for the Mission the support of spiritually minded people in many lands."[7]

The incident reflects the principles upon which both Taylor and Muller stood, their respect for each other, and, for the purposes of this book, the man Hudson Taylor.

Hudson Taylor not only emphasized God's ability to meet the needs of God's work. He was also deeply committed to the principle that God's work was to be done with quality, and that while the quality would at times be more costly, the needs would be met because they were needs sanctioned by God. Faith was the focus. Not faith abstractly without an object, but faith that God could be trusted with great tasks. For certainly one who serves a King should expect a King's supply as long as he operates under a King's command. Our King often chooses to supply us daily, momently, rather than to take away, long range, our needs. For the daily need is what keeps the focus of direction and faith upon him and his orders.

God had given Hudson Taylor great training for his life of balance in obtaining God's supply. For as the son of James Taylor he had the perfect pattern for learning both financial wisdom and godly trust.

Taylor was born to James and Amelia Taylor on May 21, 1832. He lived during the years of Charles Haddon Spurgeon, and, as has been pointed out, shared ideals with Amy Carmichael and George Muller. When he was tempted to take a more comfortable mode of travel at a higher cost—a most reasonable and justifiable action—he stated a principle regarding money with which all of these people would have agreed: "Well, it is the Lord's money, you know; we had better be very careful about it."[8] Interestingly enough, to balance out the abandon with which Hudson Taylor gave money and trusted God financially, he was no fanatic. His father's upbringing was deeply entrenched in him and is epitomized in the statement James Taylor once made regarding a bill: "If I let it stand over a week," he would say, "I defraud my creditor of interest, if only a fractional sum."[9]

James Taylor was a business man. Yet he never sued for a bill. And at times he returned in whole or in part sums that his customers could not afford. Still he was a man of so much business skill that his fellow townsmen who recognized his financial skill appointed him manager of their Building Society for a term of 22 years. It was in such an atmosphere of balance, integrity and faith that Hudson Taylor was born and grew.

Perhaps it was because he had such balance that he could afford to appear unbalanced to the world, even the Christian world. That, too, was faith. In such matters as dress his faith and sincerity were put to the acid test.

"Chinese dress and a home somewhere in the country—the thought was becoming familiar. But it was an expedient almost unheard of in those days. Sometimes on inland journeys a missionary would wear the native costume as a precautionary measure. But it was invariably discarded on the traveller's return, and he would have been careless of public opinion indeed who would have ventured to wear it always, and in the Settlement.

"But it was nothing less than this that the young missionary was meditating, driven to it by his longing to identify himself with the people and by the force of outward circumstances. If he could not find quarters in Shanghai he must go to the interior, and why add to his difficulties and hinder the work he most desired to accomplish by emphasizing the fact that he was a foreigner?"[10]

Again Taylor had an intricate balance in his life. Chinese dress was a key to his success in China. He became part of the people in a deeper way, not only because by this sign they could observe his sincerity, but because Chinese dress helped him blend into the culture rather than stand out. By his compromise in dress Taylor met the Chinese people.

Compromise has come to be a dirty word in the Christian world, although it was indeed never meant to be that. The word has become abused in our culture. Enthusiastic do-gooders smoke pot in order to reach drug addicts, or in general prostitute their principles in order to fit in with those whom they wish to help. Taylor would not have compromised principle, nor should we. But he knew the true meaning of compromise. In order to cope in China, he compromised things that had no moral overtones in order to win the very souls of people. He chanced offending his own colleagues rather than offend those among whom he lived and worked.

"Yes, it was growing clearer. For him, probably, the right thing was a closer identification with the people; Chinese dress at all times and the externals of Chinese life, including chopsticks and native cookery. How much it would simplify travelling in the interior! Already he had purchased an outfit of native clothing. If, after all the prayer there had been about it, he really could not get accommodation in Shanghai, it must be that the Lord had other purposes.

"Thursday night came. It was useless to seek premises any longer, so Hudson Taylor went down to engage the junk that was to take them to Hang-chow Bay with their belongings. His Chinese dress was ready for the following morning when he expected to begin a pilgrim life indeed. And this, apparently, was the point to which it had been necessary to lead him. He had followed faithfully. It was enough. And now on these new lines could be given the answer to weeks and months of prayer."[11]

"Later he took the step he had been prayerfully considering—called in a barber, and had himself so transformed in appearance that his own mother could hardly have known him. To put on Chinese dress without shaving the head is comparatively a simple matter; but Hudson Taylor went [to] all lengths, leaving only enough of the fair, curly hair to grow into the *queue* of the Chinaman. He had prepared a dye, moreover, with which he darkened his remaining hair, to match the long, black braid that at first must do duty for his own. Then in the morning he put on as best he might the loose, unaccustomed garments, and appeared for the first time in the gown and satin shoes of a 'Teacher,' or man of the scholarly class."[12]

As the work went on by faith, Taylor received what he needed, not always *as* he wanted or *when* it was desirable. A note dated January 27, 1874, found in the margin of his Bible reflects the proportion of his vision and the urgency of his need:

"Asked God for fifty or a hundred additional native evangelists and as many missionaries as may be needed to open up the four *Fu's* and forty-eight *Hsien* cities still unoccupied in Chekiang, also for men to break into the nine unoccupied provinces. Asked in the name of Jesus.

"'I thank thee, Lord Jesus, for the promise whereon thou has given me to rest. Give me all needed strength of body, wisdom of mind, grace of soul to do this thy so great work.'

"Yet, strange to say, the immediate sequel was not added strength, but a serious illness. Week after week he lay in helpless suffering, only able to hold on in faith to the heavenly vision. Funds had been so low for months that he had scarcely known how to distribute the little that came in, and there was nothing at all in hand for extension work. But, 'We are going on to the interior,' he had written to the secretaries in London. 'I do so hope to see some of the destitute provinces evangelized before long. I long for it by day and pray for it by night. *Can he care less?*'"[13]

Faith again was required to clarify its focus. The work was God's, Taylor was God's—and God would not fail. Taylor continued:

"Never had advance seemed more impossible. But in the Bible before him was the record of that transaction of his soul with God, and in his heart was the conviction that, even for inland China, God's time had almost come. And then as he lay there slowly recovering, a letter was put into his hands which had been two months on its way from England. It was from an unknown correspondent.

"'My dear Sir (the somewhat trembling hand had written), I bless God—in two months I hope to place at the disposal of your Council, for further extension of the China Inland Mission work, eight hundred pounds. (Then equal to about four thousand dollars, gold.) Please remember for *fresh* provinces...

"'I think your receipt-form beautiful: "The Lord our Banner"; "The Lord will provide." If faith is put forth and praise sent up, I am sure that Jehovah of Hosts will honour it.'

"Eight hundred pounds for 'fresh provinces'! Hardly could the convalescent believe he read aright. The very secrets of his heart seemed to look back at him from that sheet of foreign note paper. Even before the prayer [had been] recorded in his Bible, that letter had been sent off; and now, just when most needed, it had reached him with its wonderful confirmation. Then God's time had surely come!"[14]

And all that was true of the mission was true of God's vision for Hudson Taylor the man. For God cares about his work, but he is not some mechanistic Taskmaster who is not interested in people for themselves. Let us not forget that we are an extremely important possession of God and his care is never removed from us.

Said Taylor in a letter to his sister:

"The sweetest part, if one may speak of one part being sweeter than another, is the *rest* which full identification with Christ brings. I am no longer anxious about anything, as I realise this; for *He, I* know is able to carry out *His Will,* and His will is mine. It makes no matter where He places me, or how. That is rather for Him to consider than for me; for in the easiest positions He must give me His grace, and in the most difficult His grace is sufficient. It little matters to my servant whether I send him to buy a few cash worth of things, or the most expensive articles. In either case he looks to me for the money, and brings me his purchases. So, if God place me in great perplexity, must He not give me much guidance; in position of great

(1876–1951)

would say, 'Here are pictures of myself; I am going to leave you, you won't see me again for a little while, but I would like each of you to take one of these pictures. I wish you would cherish it and from time to time take it out and look at it, and as you do, remember me.' Would it be a task to do that in response to the request of a loving mother or a precious father or possibly a darling child? Surely not. If you loved that one, you would be delighted again and again to take down that picture and as you looked at it, you would say, 'There is the one who loved me and is now gone from me, but I call my dear one afresh to mind.' That is the place the Lord's Supper has in the Church of God. There is nothing legal about it, you do not have to participate in the Lord's Supper if you do not want to. You can go to Heaven by trusting the Saviour even if you have never once partaken of the cup that speaks of His suffering and death, but if your heart is filled with love for Him, you will be glad from time to time to gather with His people to remember Him."[1]

CHAPTER 8

Geraldine Taylor: Divine Renewal

I t was Geraldine's first year in Honan, China. She had arrived there by houseboat, traveling up the Han River in the company of Hudson Taylor's son and and his wife, Mr. and Mrs. Herbert Taylor, and their little son, Howard. It was Christmas Eve, the eve of Geraldine Guinness' own birthday and the first away from home and parents. A few days later they reached the town where they were to serve for a time, a place where no one before had ever seen a white woman.

In that first year, as she travelled from place to place, ministering to the sick and spreading the Gospel, she encountered language problems, along with cultural conflicts regarding the status and behavior of women. She lived among those who were enslaved to opium, and she learned "terrible revelations...horrible ways of sinning...and her soul had been scorched as she thought of innocent little lives cruelly sinned against. These were things she could never tell. . ."[1]

But one incident remained more agonizing than any other. A little granddaughter was given to Hudson Taylor, the daughter of his eldest son Herbert. A trained nurse had been there for the delivery, and the child was healthy and strong. Mrs. Herbert Taylor, however, was not well and required special nursing, along with the normal care required for the baby and little Howard. Geraldine, already tired and in need of medical treatment for her eyes, was needed to do her share.

Then the baby became ill with dysentery. Geraldine prepared a dose of medicine which was administered by the nurse who was there. But she had picked up the wrong bottle. Very soon the baby died. Because of the attitude of the people among whom they lived, which put no value at all on the death of a baby girl, there could be no funeral. The grief-stricken father had to bury his little daughter somewhere in Honan, in the middle of the night.

Devastated, Geraldine wrote to Hudson Taylor who was in England at the time and told him the whole story, hoping that as a physician Dr. Taylor could assure her that the baby could have died from the disease, not the medication. With characteristic wisdom, Hudson Taylor gave the letter to his son, Howard, also a doctor and a man who was very much in love with Geraldine. Otherwise the incident was kept private; and so the comfort which Howard offered to Geraldine became precious indeed and helped lead toward their marriage some five years later. Says biographer and niece Joy Guinsess: "The enemy had overreached himself, and God had overruled."[2]

"God had overruled." There was divine renewal. Baker's *Evangelical Dictionary of Theology* refers to renewal as the "reinvigorating effect of Christian committal on conduct."[3] Ephesians 4:23 reads: "And being renewed in the spirit of your mind" (Darby). H.C.G. Moule, in commenting on renewal as it is portrayed in Ephesians 4:23, states: "...as regenerated members of Christ, you have exchanged doom for peace and moral bondage for spiritual freedom..." In a further explanation of the verse, *The Expositor's Greek Testament* goes at some length to emphasize that, as Darby's translation implies, the verb here is a passive one. We do not renew ourselves; but by the Spirit of God, we are renewed. Renewal, therefore, is something which God does in us.

Pain in connection with children was something of which Geraldine had more than her share. The terrible tragedy of the loss of the Taylor baby was emphasized later on by Geraldine's own miscarriages; and, partly due to the rigors of her life in China, she was never able to bear her own children.

Because of her parents' intense involvement in missions, as a teenager Geraldine had literally raised her own younger brother and two sisters. One day her father took his little son with him when he went away to speak. Within a week the two small girls, Phoebe and Agnes, contracted diphtheria and died. Geraldine and her mother became ill with the same disease in a milder form and survived. Geraldine was just sixteen when the children died. Her grief then, as now, was sharp and deep. According to her biographer, "She never attempted to be young again."[4]

Much later in her life, when Geraldine was in her mid-forties, her sister, Lucy, died, leaving two small boys in Geraldine's care. "I want you to have Auntie Geraldine for your Mamma,"[5] Lucy wrote to the boys. And mother she was, in reality for the rest of their lives. Yet after six years, when the boys' father married again, it was right for them to be back with their father. Once again, there was a sense of wrenching loss for Geraldine.

Yet through the pain of her experiences with children Geraldine learned what it meant to be renewed. Her recovery was not that which is born of self effort: stamped with bitterness and a determination to look after *me* in the future so that I don't get hurt again. Instead the renewal came in the form of a divine tenderness and understanding.

Thirty years after her own miscarriages, the then Mrs. Howard Taylor wrote to a couple who had just buried their stillborn baby: "He called you to be a father, a mother; He gave you a precious little daughter. This can never be gone back upon. You *are* parents; the little one is yours for ever. He is keeping her for you, far more perfectly and safely than you could have kept her. And He will give her back to you when Jesus comes. Your lives are permanently enriched by all this and your usefulness for the work. The Lord has wanted this—it is part of the fruit, 'more fruit' that He has planned for your lives. How much richer and deeper now is the love with which He can love through you, the sympathy into which He can bring you with His own heart and the hearts of others...How dearly He must love you to have trusted you with this sorrow, and to have put Himself to the the grief of giving you pain. For the little life He has taken, though only to restore, may He give you many, many precious lives in His eternal kingdom."[6]

Out of deep pain had come the truest form of recovery and renewal: selflessness and abandonment to the will of God. In some paradoxical fashion her love had become gentle at the same time it dared to make demands. Hers was not a softening love. It was a love which held one to the highest. It strengthened rather than weakened. It expected the best. In the words of Amy Carmichael:

> O Father, help us lest our poor love refuse
> For our beloved the life that they would choose,
> And in our fear of loss for them, or pain,
>   Forget eternal gain.[7]

"Why *me?*" was not part of the vocabulary of Geraldine Taylor. True recovery and renewal, on the other hand, were woven throughout the fabric of her earthly life. No matter what happened she went on, and in her life story as well as in her many writings one senses the deep settled joy of the Lord. Some twelve years before her death she herself spoke of the meaning of renewal. In a journal dated July 16, 1937 she wrote:

> "Taking into account all the facts of the case,
> 'Renewed—day by day.' 2 Cor. 4:16.
> "Yes, the outward man is perishing.
> "Yes, the heart would faint.
> "Waking late this morning (6:30) after hours of sleeplessness last night, I should have been discouraged—but the Lord Himself made haste to comfort. And oh, what wealth opens up from His Word through this truth applied by His Spirit.
> Uplifting, transforming, overwhelming in grace and glory: Divine renewal.
> "'Transformed by the renewing of your mind.' Rom. 12:2.
> "'We faint not . . .though.' 4:16.
> "'While we look not at . . .but at . . .' 4:18.
> "'Strength renewed...to walk and not faint.' Is. 40:31.
> "'Always to pray...not to faint.'
>   Luke 18:1."[8]

Mary Geraldine Guinness was born to Fanny and Grattan Guiness in Waterloo, near Liverpool, on Christmas Day in the year 1862. Grattan Guinness was the son of a soldier who had died when his young son was only fourteen. Grattan Guinness went to sea at seventeen and in general sought adventure. After his conversion he developed a deep sense of the spiritual needs of others and became a preacher. Eventually, some years later he offered his services to Hudson Taylor. Since Guinness was thirty and his wife thirty-five, which Taylor felt would hinder them in developing fluency in the Chinese language, Taylor advised against it but suggested that they support missions from the home side. This the Guinness family did for the rest of their lives. All of their children went to foreign countries to do missionary work, while the parents stayed home, supported missions, and trained young missionaries.

At the time of Geraldine's birth her father had been through a period of ill health and discouragement. Grattan Guinness was a preacher who had come into fellowship with the Plymouth Brethren, a group who were at that time flourishing in England. The Brethren, noted for their deep bib-

God continued to use the China Inland Mission and He continued to use my Aunt. Recently I found a little book, published in 1898, called *Christ Our Example* by Caroline Fry. In the front page are the words:

Miss Ruth Benson
with the assurance of prayer
and remembrance of us both.
D.E. Hoste

March, 1936
"Let us consider one another to provoke
unto love and good works."

By the time my Aunt left the C.I.M. Mr. Hoste had stepped down as General Director. Apparently he did not make the final decision which related to my Aunt, since that would have occurred after 1935. But his sense of responsibility toward her, and his tender understanding of her situation, are clear in this inscription.

It takes a person finely tuned to the will of God to express kindness in the middle of disagreement. Even though he could be very firm, his suffering and life-long battle with burnout refined D.E. Hoste into a very gentle servant of God. He was continually being renewed.

In her biography of James Fraser, Geraldine shows other aspects of his life's battle against burnout. It is noteworthy that burnout is often accompanied by some psychological symptoms which were not viewed by any of these saints as sin or something to be confessed. Furthermore, burnout is viewed as something to be avoided rather than an indication of weakness or sin. "It's better to burn out rather than rust out" is not a slogan which had much appeal for these people. They were not into that kind of ego satisfaction. They did not want to be martyrs, although they would have been the first to be willing had that been the call of God for them. Many of their predecessors, along with missionaries from other missions and native Christians, had been burned with flames, cut into pieces, beheaded, and tortured with unspeakable methods in the early days of the Mission.

James Fraser opened up a ministry to the Lisu who lived high in the mountains of inland China where the Burma Road crosses through. He was young and strong, but he was also alone and pioneering areas where the gospel had never been preached. He went into areas where out and out demonism flourished. Fraser was attacking Satan's stronghold. Understandably, physical, spiritual, and emotional reactions set in. In Fraser's words: "He would be a missionary simpleton who expected plain sailing in *any* work of God."[28] Therefore, understanding the truth of Satan as a conquered foe was of primary importance.

Great men of God sometimes suffer from depression *because* they are in the center of the will of God, *not* because they have left it. In his early years of struggle with the language, along with the loneliness and physical expenditure, Fraser grappled with feelings of hopelessness, which were, at times, caused or added to by spiritual warfare. Says Geraldine: "It was not lack of interest in his surroundings that led to the depression of spirit that now began to assail him. He did not know at first what to make of it."[29] He questioned whether it could be the food, the loneliness, the drizzling mist descending over the mountains?...But as the days and weeks wore on, he realized that there were influences of another kind to be reckoned with.

"For strange uncertainty began to shadow his inward life. All he had believed and rejoiced in became unreal, and even his prayers seemed to mock him as the answers faded into nothingness...In his solitude, depression such as he had never known before closed down upon him...Deeply were the foundations shaken in those days and nights of conflict, until Fraser realized that behind it all were 'powers of darkness,' seeking to overwhelm him. He had dared to invade Satan's kingdom, undisputed for ages."[30]

In a conversation with Geraldine, Fraser explained: "I am an engineer and believe in things working. I want to see them work. I have found that much of the spiritual teaching one hears does not seem to work. My apprehension at any rate of other aspects of truth had broken down. The passive side of leaving everything to the Lord Jesus as our life, while blessedly true, was not all that was needed just then. Definite resistance on the ground of The Cross was what brought me light. For I found it worked...People will tell you, after a helpful meeting perhaps, that such and such a truth is the secret of victory. No: we need different truth at different times. 'Look to the Lord,' some will say. 'Resist the devil,' is also Scripture (James iv. 7). And I found it worked!"[31]

Listlessness and depression were common foes. But in her portrayal of Fraser, Geraldine teaches much about that sometimes confusing mass of spiritual, physical, and psychological causes. Fraser explains his approach: "I have had many such experiences (failure) before, but have made the mistake of giving way to depression instead of calmly investigating the cause of things. This time however, the thief is not going to escape..."[32]

After one such experience "Fraser came to see that it was due to physical as well as spiritual causes. He had confined himself too much to his room—the only place in which he could count on privacy—and had neglected exercise and the mental balance of good hard study. Loneliness and the pressure of surrounding darkness had driven him to his knees too exclusively. The laws of nature are also the law of God; and he had to learn that ignorance or forgetfulness of either the one or the other does not save us from the penalty of breaking them...'I now think,' he wrote quite simply, 'that a long, healthy walk was indicated, or wholesome Lisu study, rather than the "knee-drill" I practised with such signal failure.'"[33]

One of Geraldine Taylor's most successful books in terms of popular appeal was the one she wrote on Pastor Hsi, the Chinese scholar and opium addict who became a leader in the Chinese Church. It is in her portrayal of the life of this pastor that she touches on the possible exception to the usual laws of nature and God which exist in the area of burnout.

Sometimes one must simply go on, even when rational thought demands pause. During the last nine months of World War II a Swedish diplomat named Raoul Wallenberg saved 100,000 Jews in Budapest. The Jews of Europe had been scattered and systematically exterminated. This group was the one remaining major group left. There was no time to wait and there were few people to delegate work to. This was an exception to the rule against burnout.

For the Christian it is vital that any exception be one which is the distinct, personal call from God, not just the desire of some Christian leader. Each of us who tend toward over-extension can be deluded into thinking that we have this exception. "Our work is unique, special, and immediate in its demands." "There is no one else to do it." Worst, of all reasons, "We can't say 'No.'"

We have trouble separating the good from the important, the best from the better still. Most of us are not choosing between good and evil when we burn out. To the contrary, what we are doing seems so important that we feel that, just this time, God will give us extra strength. Then when He doesn't, because He does allow the laws of nature to take their course, we question His power; we say that He didn't answer prayer, or we feel weak, or we just get bitter. All this because we tried to walk on water for some reason of our own and found that, consistent with the laws of nature, we sank.

When the call to over-extension is really from God—and that will be rare indeed—I believe that it is normally for a short time, and for a specific purpose. Sometimes God will, at that time *only*, contradict the laws of nature and give extra strength and protection. It is conceivable that at other times, there will be the suffering which is the natural fallout from burnout, but that that suffering will build great treasure in eternal reward. God doesn't always make it easy to obey.

Burnout, if it is ever allowed, should never be lightly taken on, as though we believe that God will make it easy because it is His call. God enables us to do His task. He doesn't promise that there will be no pain or sacrifice. But when sacrifice is requested, the offering up of that sacrifice to God pleases Him deeply. That in itself is reward. Easy Christianity, with no pain and no sacrifice, is neither biblical nor realistic. Easy Christianity, which promises freedom from pain rather than enablement through suffering, doesn't work and simply disillusions. Like Job in the Old Testament, the sufferer is cast out by his fellows as a failure rather than viewed as one who has triumphed through his or her faith.

Pastor Hsi lived a life which was, at times, an exception to the general prohibition against burnout. In view of the future of the Chinese Church under Communist rule, Chinese Christians were to be vital to the survival and growth of that Church. And Pastor Hsi was an unusual Chinese leader who did much during his life to build that Church. His was not an ordinary life. The General Director himself, D.E. Hoste, became his intimate friend and said of him: "The more one saw of him, the more one felt that Christ had taken possession of his life—the real Christ, the living Christ."[34]

In direct relationship to over-extension, Geraldine writes: "One remarkable feature of his life, during those busy years, was the energy and endurance he manifested under long-continued strain, both mental and physical. 'I always felt,' said Mr. Hoste, who was with him constantly, 'that Hsi had a bodily strength not his own. He was a man whom God specially sustained for the work He had given him to do. I have known him to walk thirty miles at a stretch, in case of need; quite a remarkable feat for a man of his age and training; and after fasting entirely for two days, he was able to baptise by immersion as many as fifty men at one time."[35]

Perhaps consistent with this enablement,..."he was not infrequently warned of danger by a curious, sudden failure of physical strength. 'I often know,' Hsi would say, 'when special trial or temptation is at hand. I become so weak in body, that it is necessary to stop whatever I am doing, and cry to Lord,...It was not faintness exactly; but overpowering weakness, with a sense of great apprehension…Rest and food did not relieve it. But prayer always did.'"[36]

Curiously, and consistently, when he died, "there was no disease or suffering; it was just the gradual withdrawal of life, before the vital powers failed.

"'The Lord is taking away my strength,' he said. 'It must be because my work is done.'"[37]

Pastor Hsi dealt with open demon worship, opium addiction, and the warfare of unseen forces which raged against the sovereignty of God in the lives of these people. The time was short before all outside influences toward the Gospel of Jesus Christ would be shut off by the evil of Communism. God gave special resources to a surrendered human vessel through which He poured Himself out to a people who had been so long without the Gospel. In the area of burnout, Pastor Hsi's life was an exception. But no truth is complete without some discussion of exceptions, if those exceptions exist.

Whether by a wise, God-directed conservation of strength, or by the direct intervention of God in renewal and going on, Geraldine Guinness Taylor's life was one of balance and, always, recovery. In her personal life, in her work with the Chinese people, and in her task as biographer of the China Inland Mission, she knew the secret of divine renewal. Much of her going on grew out of a deep, balanced leading from God. But the true source of her power goes back to a day early in her missionary life.

Referring to herself at some special meetings which she attended in Shanghai, Geraldine wrote: "Four years in China had taught her something of the joy and blessing to be found in deeper fellowship with the Master, but something also of the deadening influences of heathenism, the powers of evil within as well as around her, the blank despair of seeking to help others when her own soul was out of living touch with Christ…Praying in anguish no one suspected for light and help, it was the last Sunday before Christmas when a word was spoken that, under God, brought deliverance and made all things new. After the evangelistic service in the C.I.M. Hall, an entire stranger—a Christian seaman—came up to her and said earnestly: 'Are you filled with the Holy Ghost?'

"Filled with the Holy Ghost? She remembered no more of the conversation, but the question burned deeper and deeper into her heart…She knew that the Holy Spirit must be her life in a certain sense, for 'if any man have not the Spirit of Christ, he is none of His.' And yet, just as certainly, she knew that she was not 'filled with the Spirit,' and was experiencing little of his power."38

Her next emotion was fear of being misled or of mistaking emotion for reality. Yet as she looked at the books of *Acts* she realized that it was full of deeds performed in the power of the Holy Spirit. According to her, "It was indeed the Holy Spirit she needed."

She saw that the Holy Spirit was a Person, to be welcomed by faith into the heart. "All the rest that can be told is that she took the step, though with fear and trembling—scarce knowing what it meant—and trusted the Holy Spirit to come in and possess her fully...Feeling nothing, realizing nothing, she just took God at His word..."39

For many months Geraldine had been troubled by her lack of power in leading people to Christ. She now prayed specifically for some conversions each day for the following week. Twenty people came to know Christ. That was *her* leading in prayer, and the request was honored.

The encouragement to Hudson Taylor was great, especially when he visited a young missionary who was dying and who had been filled with fear. When he entered her room to try to console her, he found the fear gone and the room filled with a sense of peace and triumph.

"'She told me about the Holy Spirit,' whispered the one who had so dreaded the dark valley, 'and it was just what I needed.'"

Says Geraldine: "In answer to prayer, the blessing spread."40 The members of the Mission sought the filling of the Spirit, and through divine renewal came divine power. In Hudson Taylor, as well as in the lives and work of others, the testing at times increased, but each testing became "a special opportunity for God to work and for faith to triumph."

In the middle of a severe financial need, Hudson Taylor turned to his wife and said: "Now you will watch. You will watch and see what God will do." And, according to Geraldine, there was "even a touch of joyous confidence about the words."41

Renewal had found its source. Recovery—a word so bantered about in our time—is the opposite of Me-ism when it is defined in its truest form. Recovery is to be found in "Christ-in-Me" by the power of the Holy Spirit, a recovery which at times is ministered to by the counsel and comfort of other human beings, by changed circumstances, and through appropriate medical treatment. True recovery is greater, however, than any human cure which at best simply puts the pieces back together as they were. True recovery goes further than that. It is Divine Renewal.

Arthur T. Pierson

Born in New York, Pierson became a Presbyterian minister in 1860. He was a Bible speaker, a leader at the famous Keswick Convention, and the author of many books.

"Our Father who seeks to perfect His saints in holiness knows the value of the refiner's fire. It is with the most precious metals that the assayer takes most pains, and subjects them to hot fires, because only such fires melt the metal, and only molten metal releases its alloy, or takes perfectly its new form in the mould. The old refiner never left his crucible, but sat down by it, lest there should be one excessive degree of heat to mar the metal, and so soon as, skimming from the surface the last of the dross he saw his own face reflected, he put out the fire.

"How beautifully are we told that the Redeemer 'shall sit as a Refiner and purifier of silver' (Mal. iii:3). Being determined to perfect His saints, He puts His precious Metal into His crucible. But He sits by it, and watches it. Love is His thermometer, and marks the exact degree of heat; not one

146

is manifest. When it is clear that it is given of God then we may humbly extract from it all the comfort we need."[7]

Most of us who have known the Lord for a period of time have known what it is to have a private word from the Lord. My father had a stroke in 1973 which ultimately left him unconscious and unlikely to ever recover. That was obvious to everyone involved. Yet I had a private dread of having him placed in a convalescent home and/or getting a phone call in the middle of the night telling me that he had died. I slept nervously, and went up and down between hope and despair regarding the final outcome. Then the dreaded day came when the hospital said they could do no more. We should decide, they said, what convalescent home we wanted to place him in.

That night before I went to bed I stood brushing my hair and praying out loud to God. "Do we really have to make this decision?" I asked. But as I went to sleep I realized that, for the first time in his six week long illness, my fear of telephone calls in the middle of the night was gone. At 5 am the telephone rang. Inside of me I knew what it was, but I was strangely calm. My father had gone to be with His Lord, and I was okay.

Seven years later my mother lay in a hospital room badly injured from an automobile accident. She was expected to live, however. It was mid-afternoon on Wednesday, August 13, 1980. A call from a producer at NBC came through asking me to appear on a talk show on Monday night. I hesitated. With a flash I thought: "I can't do that. That might be the day of my mother's funeral." Then, collecting myself, I thought, "How ridiculous. Your imagination is running away with you." I accepted the invitation and tried to push away all thoughts of death and funerals. But somewhere way down deep inside I wondered.

Eight hours later the phone rang. "Your mother is not doing well," a physician who happened to be in the hospital said. Quickly I went to get dressed. Within minutes the phone rang again. "Your mother is not doing well," the same voice said. Confirmed in what I had believed to be the truth when he first called, I asked: "Are you trying to tell me that she's already died?" "Yes," he replied simply. "We didn't expect this to happen." In the middle of my grief, once again I was somehow prepared, not really taken by surprise. Furthermore, no matter how hard I tried to make it a different day, the only day which was available for her funeral was Monday.

In both instances, a "private word" from the Lord had not been something to act on. It was not fortune-telling, which is condemned by God. It was something dangerously vulnerable to being affected or distorted by the emotions, by physical illness or fatigue, or by Satan, the chief liar. But in both instances, that inner preparation from God Himself had buffered the sharp edges of pain involved in the testing and was the start of inner healing and ultimate recovery. For in both intances there had been the assurance that I would be okay, even when that which I had feared from childhood, the death of my parents, really happened.

Isobel quoted Amy Carmichael with regards to this "private word": "'Before we reach the place where such waters must be crossed, there is almost always a private word spoken by the Beloved to the lover. That is the word which will be most assaulted...The enemy will fasten upon it, twist it about, belittle it, obscure it, try to undermine our confidence in its integrity, and to wreck our tranquility by making us afraid, but this will put him to flight: "I believe God that it shall be even as it was told me.""'8

For Isobel after the private word, there came the earthly reality: a diagnosis of cancer. First had come a sense that she would merely come home for a while. Then came the knowledge of the nearness of death, that "'I am getting ready to move."'9 Death became the final platform of testing. Wrote Isobel Kuhn: "For the Christian, death is not the dissolution of life but the consummation...Or as Amy Carmichael words it, 'The days of our bloom and our power are just about to begin.'"

> Gone, they tell me, is youth;
> Gone is the strength of my life.
> Nothing remains but decline,
> Nothing but age and decay.
>
> Not so, I'm God's little child,
> Only beginning to live.
> Coming the days of my prime,
> Coming the strength of my life,
> Coming the vision of God,
> Coming my bloom and my power![10]

Isobel Kuhn thought of all of life's difficulties as a platform upon which God shows Himself. For Isobel, as for most of us, one of these platforms was that of physical and emotional stress and illness. Hudson Taylor had once said: "Difficulties afford a platform upon which He can show Himself."[11]   The verse which occurred to Isobel when she was thinking about such platforms was: "'For I think that God hath set forth us...last...for we are made a spectacle unto the world (I Cor. 4:9).'"[12]

In further explanation she added: "The Word says that we will be a theatron to men and angels. Some of our most painful platforms may have no human witness. In that case we should remember the significant words, *and angels*. I'm sure that the suffering of the saints, while its purpose is to teach us more of Himself, to develop and enrich us, also bears fruit in other lives..."[13]

In a Preface to Isobel Kuhn's book *Green Leaf in Drought Time*, J. Oswald Sanders explains the concept of platform using the word testing. "God does not waste suffering," says Sanders, "nor does He discipline out of caprice. If He plows, it is because He purposes a crop. . . life apparently is meant to be a series of tests in the school of God. The tests He sends or permits are in reality His vote of confidence, for He undertakes not to allow us to suffer any testing beyond our powers of endurance.[14]

Before Isobel Kuhn was a missionary and a writer she was a teacher. Born in 1901 she married John Kuhn after leaving teaching in order to be a missionary to China under the CIM. Additionally, Isobel wrote a number of books relating to their missionary work and that of the Mission in general. Many of these books are highly devotional as well as biographical and autobiographical.

For a number of years John and Isobel Kuhn served as missionaries to the Lisu in China, continuing the work of James Fraser who had died and developing their own work. Later, after the Communists took over China, and the China Inland Mission changed its name to Overseas Missionary Fellowship, they served in Thailand under the OMF until Isobel's death in 1957.

Before I was a family counselor and a writer, I, like Isobel Kuhn, was a teacher. To me, therefore, and obviously to her, it makes sense that a discussion of any individual Christian life could be effectively expressed in the testings which comprise that life as well as in the principles upon which it is built.

The word *testing* contains many connotations. We test products, like lawn mowers and chairs, to make sure they work and endure. We test drugs and foods for their safety and purity. We test gold for its value and gems for their authenticity. Testing is a major factor which insures quality in the commercial realm.

This is true in the human realm as well. We test children in school. We each have to pass a test to drive, or to obtain a certain license or credential to do a job. We test people for physical illnesses or mental disorders. We judge quality by these tests. We show excellence as well as discover problems by such tests.

In God's school testing goes one step further. By testing, by using various platforms in which to manifest Himself, God develops us and makes us exactly what He wants us to be in order to fulfill our role on this earth as well as prepare for our role in Heaven.

Just as problems relating to physical health and healing were platforms of testing throughout Isobel Kuhn's life, the correct valuation of things was another area which was tested. At the outset of her missionary career the General Director of the CIM Mr. Hoste had said: "Miss Miller, if I had a beautiful bedspread, I would throw it in the river." Says Isobel: "I was startled. Did he have X-ray eyes? I did have a beautiful quilt in my boxes, a wedding gift from a girl friend. But how did Mr. Hoste know that? And if he did, why should he object?"[15]

Later she understood his remarks. Following her marriage to John, just after she had fixed up their little home as attractively as possible, they had guests from the church where they ministered. The guests admired the pretty things. But then, to Isobel's horror, an elderly woman "blew her nose with her fingers, and—wiped the stuff off on my beautiful traveling rug! In another minute a young mother laughingly held her baby son out over my new rattan rug. She carried him to the door, but as she went she carefully held him out over the rug so that a wet streak ran down the center of my cherished floor covering. Since their own floors were of earth my visitor had no idea that she was doing anything offensive to me."[16]

Outwardly Isobel remained courteous, but after the guests left, "I returned to my deflated sitting room and stood looking at it—that disgusting gob on my traveling rug and the discolored streak across the pretty new mat. Hot resentment rose in my heart, and then there followed my first battle over things.

"Suddenly I understood what Mr. Hoste had meant: 'Miss Miller, if I had a beautiful bedspread, I would throw it into the river.' He did not mean that he did not like beautiful things. He meant that if possessions would in any way interfere with our hospitality, it would be better to consign them to the river. In other words, if your finery hinders your testimony, throw it out. In our Lord's own words, if thine hand offend thee, cut it off; He was not against our possessing hands, but against our using them to hold on to sinful or hindering things.

"So I faced my choice. In our first home—what was to come first? An attractive sitting room just for ourselves? Or a room suited to share with the local Chinese? ...Mentally I offered that pretty rattan furniture to the Lord to be wrecked by the country peasants if they chose..."[17]

After Isobel had been in China for a number of years she and her husband came home to the United States. In her words: "...we were invited to a house, a house beautifully decorated and furnished with all that modern art and household conveniences can offer. The two who owned it had no children. They both worked all day and could use their house only at nights and on holidays. As we were shown through its perfectly ordered, spotlessly clean rooms, where two human lives were being spent just in order to maintain these things, a desolating sense of barrenness swept over me. What a terrible waste! Two lives spent for just this....I felt what an aching tragedy those two barren human lives were—all their God-given sympathies, energizing love, and passion spent on things. Physical hardship and spiritual luxury; physical comfort and spiritual death. Oh, that we would waken to the real values of life."[18]

On another occasion, once again on a furlough home, Isobel relates a similar incident: "I met a lady who said to me, 'I have no interest in anything but my house and my garden. My house and my garden are my life.' I thought how pitifully poor she had confessed herself to be; even though hers was a large expensive house and mine a mere shanty on the wild mountain side...And my heart cried out, 'What a waste! for her to spend that human life and sympathies on a wooden house and a dirt garden when God's spiritual house is calling out for living stones and His garden has Seedlings of Eternal Destiny that need to be trained!' But America is full of human beings (church-goers, many of them) who live just for things. When that lady dies, she must leave behind her house and her garden— everything that spells life to her by her own confession...What are you living for—what is your life?"[19]

At the end of the twentieth century we human beings seem to be more thing-conscious than ever. More than ever we seem to judge success by money, fame, power, and possessions. Character, kindness, and sacrifice are not popular as goals. The rot is in us all. Sometimes I feel defeated and defensive because I don't have the big home and the expensive car. To be honest all I really want in a car is safety and durability. A bigger place to live is becoming important to me for some good, practical reasons, but I can live without it, and I can do God's work without it.

Not long ago a friend shared a thought with me which has stayed in my mind. We were talking about *things*, and he cited Bishop Fulton Sheen as having stated that in the area of clothing the quality and type, as well as the quantity of clothing which any one individual possesses, should be appropriate to the vocation or occupation of that person. It made sense. After all a big game hunter in Africa would not need the perfect dress clothes of a conductor of the New York Philharmonic.

The danger is that even we Christians tend to judge our work for God by how splashy it is, how prosperous we look. *Things* become status symbols. Yet we, above all others, know that we are only a heartbeat away from Heaven where all that will count is how much we built in the gold, silver, and precious stones of Heaven, not the wood, hay, and stubble of earth. Only that which is eternal really matters. In Isobel Kuhn's words: "Lisuland is a place of physical hardship and spiritual luxury, but if you have ever tasted that luxury all else will be tame ever after."[20]

There is another testing which goes beyond the testing of things. That is the testing of that which we are willing to suffer for His sake. Such testing was another platform in the life and ministry of Isobel Kuhn.

One Christmas night, high up in those mountainous precipices of Lisuland, Isobel was asked to give the message to the little group which had gathered. She took as her theme: "And when they had opened their treasures, they presented unto him gifts; gold, and frankincense, and myrrh.

"Gold represents our wealth, the possession we may offer to our King. Frankincense is a type of our worship. But the myrrh? That bitter thing? Surely that can have only one meaning—the things we are willing to suffer for His sake. We were all bringing our gold to Him, making our freewill offerings. Some were also bringing a bit of frankincense. But was anyone bringing Him myrrh?

"As I put the question, one face in the audience stood out sharply, a lean brown face with understanding eyes that burned with hot tears. He was one who had been beaten by the feudal lord because he had become a Christian, beaten so mercilessly that he could not walk for three days. Yes, in that faraway rim of the earth, among those poor and ragged tribespeople in their barren mountains, there were offerings of myrrh that Christmas time.

"'Lord, I bring Thee my myrrh.' That was the silent heart-cry that had taken the hurt and fear out of our journey to Lisuland. I had seldom before been able to offer Him that gift, and I have never forgotten the joy of it."[21]

In making application of the concept of myrrh to those of us who live in this country, Isobel asks: "Isn't the coldness in our churches today due to the fact that we offer Christ only our gold? We have for a long time ceased to offer Him myrrh."[22] Then putting the idea into shoeleather: "Most myrrh is undramatic. There are those who would be willing to be beaten for Christ's sake or willing to climb over landslides, but yet would be quite unwilling to spend half an hour daily in prayer for His cause and His kingdom. It is myrrh when you say quietly to a pressing friend, 'No, I cannot go tonight—there is something I must do,' and then spend that time in intercession...The cost of myrrh is monotony and obscurity...Lord, I bring Thee my myrrh."[23] The bringing of myrrh is another testing ground, another platform of exhibit for the world to see and for the encouragement of angels.

All of us have our special platforms for testing. Relationships with parents, spouses, children; marriage; choice of a life work; daily organization of our lives and work; hospitality; financial loss or gain; rejection: these and many more can become situations of testing. They can become platforms for glory or doom. The life of Isobel Kuhn reads like the story of a pilgrim, a sort of modern Pilgrim's Progress, if you life.

In Hebrews 11:13 we are called "pilgrims on the earth," "sojourners among aliens." Weymouth adds: "For men who acknowledge this make it manifest that they are seeking elsewhere a country of their own." This world is truly not our Home, but it is a testing place of importance to all eternity. We are being tested and shaped in the school of God.

Testing in the school of God rests upon living in the truth of certain biblical principles which God has shown in His word and through the lives of His saints. One of the strengths of Isobel Kuhn's writing lies in her ability to present concise principles for godly living which God made real to her. Which principles stand out in any individual life may vary according to our personality as well as our calling.

In talking about scriptural principles, Isobel Kuhn often uses imagery, particularly imagery relating to gemstones. Using a quote from G. Campbell Morgan she explains: "'What a strange bringing together of contradictions! "Stones of fire." A stone is the last embodiment of principle—hard and cold. Fire is the essence of passion—warm and energizing. Put the two together, and we have stones—principle; fire—passion; principle shot through with passion, passion held by principle.'"24 In God's King-dom we are, indeed, living stones made up of passion and principle.

Once again using a quote regarding gemstones to illustate a slightly dif-ferent slant on the same idea: "'Do you know that lovely fact about the opal? That in the first place, it is made only of desert dust, sand, and silica, and owes its beauty and preciousness to a defect. It is a stone with a broken heart. It is full of minute fissures which admit air, and the air refracts the light. Hence its lovely hues and that sweep lamp of fire that ever burns at its heart, for the breath of the Lord God is in it.

"'You are only conscious of the cracks and desert dust, but so He makes His precious opal. We must be broken in ourselves before we can give back the lovely hues of His light, and the lamp in the temple can burn in us and never go out.'"25

Passion held by principle involves perfect balance: not the coldness of straight principle, nor the uncontrolled emotion of total passion. When our feelings, our passions, even our godly passions, become the overwhelming force in our lives, we need to apply principle. When principle leaves us cold and unfeeling and even legalistic, we need to infuse that principle with passion. The following are a few of the basic principles which appear in the writing of Isobel Kuhn.

When tempted to sink in the face of difficulties:

By quoting G. Campbell Morgan Isobel Kuhn offers a scriptural princi-ple which is simple but widespread in its application: "'The whole differ-ence between faith and fear is that of the difference of putting our "buts" before or after God. God commands, but there are difficulties. That is paral-ysis. There are difficulties, but God commands. That is power.' So," says Isobel Kuhn, "we shook off our paralysis and deliberately placed the *but* before God."26

When tempted to rush guidance:

"Someone has said, 'Satan rushes men. God leads them.'" And Dr. F.B. Meyer has these potent words on the subject: 'Never act in panic, nor allow man to dictate to thee; calm thyself and be still; force thyself into the quiet of thy closet until the pulse beats normally and the scare has ceased to dis-turb. When thou art most eager to act is the time when thou wilt make the most pitiable mistakes. Do not say in thine heart what thou wilt or wilt not do, but wait upon the God until He makes known His way. So long as that way is hidden, it is clear that there is not need of action, and that He accounts Himself responsible for all the results of keeping thee where thou art.'"27

Offering a further principle regarding guidance, Isobel speaks of a time when "He had given me no Bible verse on which to lean. I had asked for one but none came. It would have been so comfortable to have a Bible verse to stand upon" as in an earlier time. But "God expects His children to grow. I believe it was D.E. Hoste who said that the older he grew the harder it seemed to get guidance from the Lord. I believe he meant that guidance becomes less simple. God expects us to exercise spiritual discernment, and He guides by a certain pressure on the spirit, by a still small voice, by a something so delicately intangible that unless you are carefully tuned in to His Spirit, so to speak, you can miss it widely. It requires a close and experienced walk with the Lord, so in one sense, He has a hold on us that might not be if He always supplied us with a Bible verse every time we asked for one!

"When it is only a still small voice which is our guide, it is easy for Satan to throw us into confusion by causing us to question if we heard aright. It is a good plan not to go back on past guidance."28

When tempted to imagine the worst:

When Isobel Kuhn came back to the United States due to cancer, a whole new platform of testing began—and the need for principle which would control emotion. In her book *In the Arena* she cited the verse from II Corinthians 10:5: "...casting down imaginations...and bringing into captivity every thought to the obedience of Christ."

In commenting on that verse she wrote: "I found that imagination could give me a bad time. If I coughed, for instance, I immediately had lung cancer (although X-rays showed the chest to be clear)! If I had a toothache, then I was getting cancer of the mouth! And so on. Every tickle or twinge was instantly interpreted as related to my grim enemy. But if I asserted my right to a sound mind (II Timothy 1:7), these fears left me and the twinges never developed into anything further. 'For God hath not given us the spirit of fear, but of power and of love and of a sound mind.' A sound mind is our gift from God, this verse says, but we need to claim it. The American Standard Version translates that word as discipline. And the one includes the other, for a sound mind is necessarily a disciplined one."[29] Discipline is a principle of Christian living.

For me personally this verse and others like it always seemed impossible to put into action until I viewed the "What-ifs" as tapes, which, when they play out of control, can throw any of us into chaos and panic. To *cut* those tapes, to literally take the tape out of the mental tape recorder, and *refocus* by playing a new positive tape is my way of exercising mental discipline on my "What-ifs." It is one way to put this biblical principle into shoeleather. Indeed, it is a very important principle, for if one problem more than any other troubles people who come to me for counseling it is the problem of negative tapes.

When tempted to feel overwhelmed:

When Arthur and Wilda Mathews were imprisoned by the Communists in China, Arthur said: "We have His promise, we are not the prey of the terrible. We are the prisoners of the Lord Jesus Christ—just lent to evil men to show forth the abundance of His power! Our days are on deposit with Him; let Him hand them out to use as He will."[30] It is a principle of living the Christian life that God is in control.

In her own troubles Isobel found great comfort in "the gathering of the edelweiss of God. I owe this thought to Miss Carmichael. In her book *Gold by Moonlight*, she has a whole chapter on it. Edelweiss grows on barren mountain heights, and its soft beauty is a cheery surprise to the toiling climber. So Miss Carmichael likens it to the little things of joy which can always be found in any painful experience, if we only gather them as we go along. Sound health and a normal life I cannot have while on this platform (cancer); therefore I accept the fact and do not fret about it. But this very trial has brought me unexpected joys and these I dwell on and delight in them as His kind tokens of remembrance..."[31]

In talking about the fear of leaving loved ones behind when she dies, she concludes that the same loving God who gives her constant small tokens of His love, will not forget them either. Then quoting Amy Carmichael:

> For my beloved I will not fear: Love knows to do
> For him, for her, from year to year, as hitherto;
> Whom my heart cherishes are dear
> To Thy heart too.[32]

Ultimately, too, Isobel concludes: "It may not be long before He comes for all His own—then what a foolish waste fretting about it would have been."[33]

Once again speaking of small comforts Isobel quotes words from Oswald Chambers which were a comfort to Wilda Mathews during her imprisonment in China: "The things that make God dear to us are not as much His great big blessings as the tiny things; because they show His amazing intimacy with us; He knows every detail of our individual lives."[34] For Wilda, the "tiny thing" was the ability to give a little birthday party for her child, in spite of their confinement.

When tempted to underestimate the power of prayer:

Before Isobel Kuhn ever went to China, she went to a Bible Conference where she heard the speaker, James Fraser. At the time she didn't dream of the effect that unknown man would have on her life, and that of her husband, John, whom she had not even met yet. Still certain words which he said remained in her mind forever. "One lecture was on the spiritual battle in the heavenlies. How he roughed it, and labored, and had given them [the Lisu tribes] a written language—and still there were so few converts and such as did come were not stable. Then he wrote his mother in England to gather in the neighbors and pray. It was only after this prayer group began to function in earnest that "the break" came in the Lisu tribe. At that time he on the field had been led to resist in Christ's name the devil and his host who were holding this tribe enchained.

"As I sat listening," wrote Isobel, "I saw plainly that it was true the Lisu church was born in prayer travail, and I decided that I must also employ this weapon of 'all-prayer.' It is so obviously effective and is attainable to any of us. I received a life-pattern at that moment for which I have ever been grateful."[35]

On another occasion she learned another lesson in prayer from James Fraser. In the middle of frustrations, "those that are from the Devil we must refuse in Christ's name. Mr. Fraser taught us to pray, 'If it is from the Devil I refuse it and all his works in Christ's name.'"[36] There is a parallel to these words to be found in the writings of John Bunyan: "If it be of God, let me not despise it; if it be of the Devil, let me not embrace it."[37]

When tempted to underestimate Satan's attack:

Isobel relates a time at the same Bible conference where she heard James Fraser speak on prayer when she was able to talk privately to him about her own call to China. She never forgot that time, sitting alone with him on a rocky shore by the ocean.

"'Missionary life can be very lonely,' he said quietly, and then he proceeded to unfold some of his own early sufferings. I believe now that he did it deliberately to sift me. If I were truly called of God, I would not be discouraged by plain talk about the cost. If I were not called by God, but just had romantic notions about a foreign land, the sooner my gossamer dream wafted away the better. But he little knew the unveiling of his own life that he was giving unconsciously. In fact, as he reminisced he seemed to forget for a while that I was present. His blue-grey eyes brooding out over the sunny, sparkling ocean, he seemed almost to be talking to himself. In the quiet of contemplation, as now, his eyes seemed to reveal an understanding of all the sorrows and loneliness that a human heart can know. Acquainted with grief, they were sad eyes; knowing the victory possible, they were steadfast and patient.

"I told him of Mother's viewpoint and her opposition to my call. He answered with the slow drawl which was his when thinking out a question—for none could talk faster than he on occasion: 'I have sensed that Satan is opposing you and working through your mother and your brother. We are taught "whom resist" when it comes to obstacles produced by the devil. I think that should be your stand. In prayer resist the devil, always remembering to be kind to those who are unconsciously his tools at the moment. II Timothy 2:24. I have a prayer-formula which I use on such occasions. It is this: "If this obstacle be from Thee, Lord, I accept it: but if it be from Satan, I refuse him and all his works in the name of Calvary. I have found that this formula works."' I was to use it throughout my life and never found it to fail when prayed with the honest intention of obeying all that it implied."[38]

Then with a prophetic note he warned her that even after she got to Bible school, Satan might try to stop her. "I wonder if you will ever get to China," he said thoughtfully. "You are very young and you have great obstacles to face." He warned her that if she ever got a telegram urging her to go home immediately because of the illness of her mother she should not immediately leave.[39] Instead she should consult with someone who was unprejudiced and yet godly enough to advise her.

Because of that warning from Fraser, when his prophetic word came true and the telegram came regarding her father's illness, not her mother's, she was prepared. It turned out that Isobel could stay in school, and her father went on to live for nearly twenty years more. Because of the godly insight and counsel of James Fraser, Satan's attempt to end the life work of Isobel Kuhn was defeated. She did, indeed, get to China, and in her short life she left behind a legacy of writing as well.

When tempted to withdraw from the unloveable:

In speaking of Christ's love, Isobel Kuhn used the words of F.B. Meyer: "You would like to love with a strong, undying flame—but perhaps you fail to distinguish between love and the emotion of love. They are not the same. We may love without being directly conscious of love...they love who obey."[40]

When speaking of the unloveable and the need for actual physical contact in dealing with them, she quotes Hudson Taylor: "'There is a mighty power in contact...They are not clean, and sometimes we are tempted to draw our skirts together; but I believe there is no blessing when that is the case...There is much power in drawing near to this people, and there is a wonderful power in touching people. A poor woman in Cheng-tu when she heard of Mrs. Riley's death said, "What a loss to us! She used to take hold of my hand, and comfort me so..." If you put your hand on the shoulder of a man there is power in it...there is something in contact: it is a real power we may use for God.'"[41]

In his book *Life in Christ* John Stott gives a remarkable example on the subject of the kind of love which touches the untouchable: "What is Mother Teresa's secret? On a board in the parlour of the Mother House in Calcutta are inscribed her own words: 'Let each sister see Jesus Christ in the person of the poor; the more repugnant the work or the person, the greater also must be her faith, love and cheerful devotion in ministering to our Lord in this distressing disguise.' Desmond Doig describes his first memory of her in Nirmal Hriday, her home for dying destitutes in Kalighat, under the shadow of the Temple of Kali. She was kneeling beside a dying man whom she had just admitted. 'Stripped of his rags, he was one appalling wound alive with maggots.' What did Mother Teresa do? She fell on her knees beside him. Then 'with quiet efficiency she began to clean him as she talked to him caressingly in Bengali.' A young Indian called Christo Das joined her, and then took over. When he had finished he said: 'When I cleanse the wounds of the poor, I am cleansing the wounds of Christ.' He had learned this from Mother Teresa, for she has written: 'I see Christ in every person I touch, because he has said "I was hungry, I was thirsty, I was naked, I was sick, I was suffering, I was homeless…" It is as simple as that. Every time I give a piece of bread, I give it to him.'"[42]

When tempted to feel that God has forgotten:

In quoting once again from Wilda Mathews during her imprisonment under the Communists, Isobel Kuhn gives a valuable help to those who might feel forgotten of God, or wonder why He has not answered prayer in the way that they might wish: "Another great help was on Hebrews 11:39. [Someone has put it in a free paraphrase] 'They were trusted to trust without receiving what others received. They were trusted not to be offended.' How I pray that I may not be offended in the least bit! He could have gotten us home in time. There is much He could have done and yet He hasn't. Oh, may my heart truly be able to say 'not my will but thine be done.'

> Teach us in the silence of the Unexplained
> To see Love's dearest, Love's most secret sign;
> Like the White Stone, a precious thing unstained,
> And as at Bethany, the glory Thine."

In the words of Wilda's husband, Arthur: "'The silence of eternity, Interpreted by love…' We trust your love has been able to find the right interpretation."[43] It is a principle of God that God is no man's debtor, that He can truly *never* make a mistake. To rest in the unexplained is perhaps one of the highest tests this earth can offer.

When tempted to give up:

Once more on the backdrop of the imprisonment of the Mathews' family, Isobel Kuhn quotes, this time from Andrew Murray, and in so doing gives us a concise and valuable principle for dealing with discouragement: "In commerce, in study, in war it is so often said: there is no safety but in advance…To stand still is to go back. To cease effort is to lose ground. To slacken the pace, before the goal is reached, is to lose the race."[44]

Arthur Mathews adds a note of additional wisdom: "The yoke is *light* only as it is *taken*, and not as it is *suffered*."[45]

When tempted to view the Christian life as one of ease:

In a day of easy Christianity, when becoming a Christian is viewed by some as simply a passport to Heaven or a way to become successful on this earth, whatever is meant by the word success, the challenge and demands of Christianity remain the same as they have always been. There is nothing on this earth to compare with the joy of belonging to the King of Kings. But the price tag of such belonging is still the Cross. And the obligation of those so purchased is still total committal to the Lordship of Christ. We are not saved by works, but the reality of our faith is made evident by our works. The words of Samuel Rutherford, quoted in Carolyn Canfield's biography of Isobel Kuhn, remain true today as much or more than in the day when they were written:

> "Ye will not get leave to steal quickly to Heaven, in Christ's company, without a conflict and a cross."[46]

But oh what a joy it will be when after the conflict and the cross there will be the crown and the "Well done thou good and faithful servant." In the words of Amy Carmichael, whom Isobel Kuhn loved so much, words which have come true for Isobel: "What an awakening one who has walked with Him in the twilight must have, when suddenly she awakes in His likeness and the light is shining round her—all shadowy ways forgotten."[47]

George MacDonald

A devout Scotsman and an author of a large number of novels, George MacDonald became a strong influence on C.S. Lewis.

Of children: "To require of a child only what he can understand the reason of, is simply to help to make himself his own God—that is a devil."[1]

Of the home: "It is not house, and fire, and plenty of servants, and all the things that money can procure, that make a home—not father or mother or friends—but one heart which will not be weary of helping, will not be offended with the petulance of sickness, nor the ministrations needful to weakness. This 'entire affection hating nicer hands' will make a home of a cave in a rock, or a gipsy's tent. *David Elginbrod,* Book III, XXI"[2]

Of whether or not we can pray for those who have gone on to Heaven before us: "'Then where would be the harm if you were to pray for me after I am gone?'

'No where that I know. It were indeed a strange thing if I might pray for you up to the moment when you ceased to breathe, and therewith an iron gate closed between us, and I could not even reach you through the ear of the Father of us both! It is a faithless doctrine, for it supposes either that

CHAPTER 10

C.S. Lewis: Dealing with Imperfection

"I f I were to say what I really thought about pain, I should be forced to make statements of such apparent fortitude that they would become ridiculous if anyone knew who made them."[1] So wrote C.S. Lewis— scholar, teacher, former professor of Medieval and Renaissance English at Cambridge University—with an honesty about his inner feelings which could only characterize a person with great strength, a person strong enough to face his imperfection.

Showing himself as a man of contrasts, in speaking of the awesomeness of God, Lewis found his modern example in a child's story, The Wind in the Willows, where Rat and Mole approach Pan on the island:

> "'Rat,' he found breath to whisper, shaking, 'Are you afraid?' 'Afraid?' murmured the Rat, his eyes shining with unutterable love. 'Afraid? of Him? O, never, never. And yet—and yet—O Mole, I am afraid.'"[2]

Other theologians and philosophers might find their examples only in the profound utterances of ancient thinkers. Lewis could find depth of expression in the simplicity of a child's story.

And so was the man Lewis: intellectual, but human; fearful, yet honest; questioning, yet believing; human and imperfect like the rest of us. Yet in all of his strength and at times weakness, he was honest enough to admit to the imperfection which existed in himself and in the rest of mankind. He could accept imperfection as just that: neither virtue nor sin but human frailty. While volumes have been written on C.S. Lewis, the intellectual, the strain of humanity which exists throughout all of his writings, and especially in his letters, has been neglected.

Many misconceptions regarding imperfection and sin persist about those who seek professional counseling. The least accurate and most unsophisticated misconception is that a person consults a psychological counselor when one is crazy. The idiocy of that statement is self-evident. More subtle is the notion in the mind of some Christians that if people would just confess their sins their problems would vanish, the idea being that sin is at the root of most emotional problems. Unfortunately, there are writers whose works reflect this erroneous concept.

To the contrary, most people who consult me with their emotional problems have difficulties which could not accurately be labeled as sinful. Anxiety, depression, sexual problems and the other difficulties which confront a counselor are certainly human imperfections, but hardly sins. The sin label not only makes the problem harder to bear because it adds the dimension of guilt, but also because it frequently hinders people from getting much needed help. For, in a sense, getting psychological help becomes an admission of guilt.

We are all imperfect. And when any imperfection becomes overwhelming we may need professional help. But what we do not need is theological put-downs, declarations of our sinfulness and inadequacy. "Be ye perfect," is a valid scriptural principle, but it is also a call to wholeness, to completeness. It is not a denial of man's inevitable imperfection.

"You would like to know how I behave when I am experiencing pain, not writing books about it? You need not guess, for I will tell you; I am a great coward. But what is that to the purpose? When I think of pain—of anxiety that gnaws like fire and loneliness that spreads out like a desert, and the heartbreaking routine of monotonous misery, or again of dull aches that blacken our whole landscape or sudden nauseating pains that knock a man's heart out at one blow, of pains that seem already intolerable and then are suddenly increased, of infuriating scorpion-stinging pains that startle into maniacal movement a man who seemed half dead with his previous tortures—it 'quite o'ercrows my spirit.' If I knew any way of escape I would crawl through sewers to find it. But what is the good of telling you about my feelings? You know them already: they are the same as yours. I am not arguing that pain is not painful. Pain hurts. That is what the word means. I am only trying to show that the old Christian doctrine of being made 'perfect through suffering' is not incredible. To prove it palatable is beyond my design."[3]

Again, this time in relationship to anaesthetics, Lewis described the same fears:

> "My reason is perfectly convinced by good evidence that anaesthetics do not smother me and that properly trained surgeons do not start operating until I am unconscious. But that does not alter the fact that when they have me down on the table and clap their horrible mask over my face, a mere child-ish panic begins inside me. I start thinking I am going to choke, and I am afraid they will start cutting me up before I am properly under. In other words, I lose my faith in anaesthetics."[4]

How many times do we fear pain before that pain occurs? I dreaded the phone call from the hospital announcing my father's death for weeks before it occurred. I feared it. Yet when the call came, I handled it. I didn't crumble, become hysterical, or do any of the things my imagination had conjured up. I absorbed the shock for a little while, cooked breakfast for my mother and sister, and helped with funeral arrangements. Often our anticipated fear of physical and emotional pain outdoes its reality. But again, we are human and so we fear pain.

When questioned about suffering by one who suggested that a good God will not inflict pain, Lewis replied:

"What do people mean when they say, 'I am not afraid of God because I know He is good?' Have they never even been to a dentist?"[5]

At the epitome of his life-pain, his grief over the death of Joy, his wife of three years, Lewis wrote not only of the pain he was feeling in handling this blow, but also of his doubt that he would ever totally recover:

"Getting over it so soon? But the words are ambiguous. To say the patient is getting over it after an operation for appendicitis is one thing; after he's had his leg off it is quite another. After that operation either the wounded stump heals or the man dies. If it heals, the fierce, continuous pain will stop. Presently he'll get back his strength and be able to stump about on his wooden leg. He has 'got over it.' But he will probably have recurrent pains in the stump all his life, and perhaps pretty bad ones; and he will always be a one-legged man. There will be hardly any moment when he forgets it. Bathing, dressing, sitting down and getting up again, even lying in bed, will all be different. His whole way of life will be changed. All sorts of plea-sures and activities that he once took for granted will have to be simply written off. Duties too. At present I am learning to get about on crutches. Perhaps I shall presently be given a wooden leg. But I shall never be a biped again."[6]

In severe psychological pain the feeling that things will never be normal again is usual. A depressed lady who consulted me, after seeing several other therapists, kept saying, "I have a hard time coming here because I keep feeling that nothing can help." Lewis would have understood her feelings.

In a profoundly sympathetic view of the potential despair in everyone as well as in himself, Lewis exclaimed in his initial grief over Joy's death:

> "They say an unhappy man wants distractions—something to take him out of himself. Only as a dog-tired man wants an extra blanket on a cold night; he'd rather lie there shivering than get up and find one. It's easy to see why the lonely become untidy; finally, dirty and disgusting."[7]

Of Niceness and Nastiness

And thus as he was realistic about himself, so he was equally aware of the frailties of mankind in general. His description of the questionable "niceness" of Christians in *Mere Christianity* says it well:

> "We must, therefore, not be surprised if we find among the Christians some people who are still nasty. There is even, when you come to think it over, a reason why nasty people might be expected to turn to Christ in greater numbers than nice ones. That was what people objected to about Christ during his life on earth; he seemed to attract 'such awful people.' That is what people still object to, and always will. Do you not see why? Christ said, 'Blessed are the poor' and, 'How hard it is for the rich to enter the Kingdom,' and no doubt he primarily meant the economically rich and economically poor. But do not his words also apply to another kind of riches and poverty? One of the dangers of having a lot of money is that you may be quite satisfied with the kinds of happiness money can give and so fail to realize your need for God. If everything seems to come simply by signing checks, you may forget that you are at every moment totally dependent on God. Now quite plainly, natural gifts carry with them a similar danger. If you have sound nerves and intelligence and health and popularity and a good upbringing, you are likely to be quite satisfied with your character as it is. 'Why drag God into it?' you may ask. A certain level of good conduct comes fairly easily to you. You are not one of those wretched creatures who are always being tripped up by sex, or dipsomania, or nervousness, or bad temper. Everyone says you are a nice chap and (between ourselves) you

agree with them. You are quite likely to believe that all this niceness is your own doing; and you may easily not feel the need for any better kind of goodness. Often people who have all these natural kinds of goodness cannot be brought to recognize their need for Christ at all until, one day, the natural goodness lets them down and their self-satisfaction is shattered. In other words, it is hard for those who are 'rich' in this sense to enter the Kingdom.

"It is very different for the nasty people—the little, low, timid, warped, thin-blooded, lonely people, or the passionate, sensual, unbalanced people. If they make any attempt at goodness at all, they learn, in double quick time, that they need help. It is Christ or nothing for them. It is taking up the cross and following—or else despair. They are the lost sheep; He came specially to find them. They are (in one very real and terrible sense) the 'poor': He blessed them. They are the 'awful set' He goes about with—and of course the Pharisees say still, as they said from the first, 'If there were anything in Christianity those people would not be Christians.'

"There is either a warning or an encouragement here for every one of us. If you are a nice person—if virtue comes easily to you—beware! Much is expected from those to whom much is given. If you mistake for your own merits what are really God's gifts to you through nature, and if you are contented with simply being nice, you are still a rebel; and all those gifts will only make your fall more terrible, your corruption more complicated, your bad example more disastrous. The Devil was an archangel once; his natural gifts were as far above yours as yours are above those of a chimpanzee.

"But if you are a poor creature—poisoned by a wretched upbringing in some house full of vulgar jealousies and senseless quarrels—saddled, by no choice of your own, with some loathsome sexual perversion—nagged day in and day out by an inferiority complex that makes you snap at your best friends—do not despair. He knows all about it. You are one of the poor whom He blessed. He knows what a wretched machine you are trying to drive. Keep on. Do what you can. One day (perhaps in another world, but perhaps far sooner than that) He will fling it on the scrap-heap and give you a new one. And then you may astonish us all—not least yourself: for you have learned your driving in a hard school. (Some of the last will be first and some of the first will be last.)

"'Niceness'—wholesome, integrated personality—is an excellent thing. We must try by every medical, educational, economic, and political means in our power to produce a world where all have plenty to eat. But we must not suppose that even if we succeeded in making everyone nice we should have saved their souls. A world of nice people, content in their own niceness, looking no further, turned away from God, would be just as desperately in need of salvation as a miserable world—and might even be more difficult to save."[8]

Most of us know that Christians are not all nice but we find it a fact which is hard to admit to. We even know on a gut level that we are not always nice, and that is even harder for us to accept.

A Christian businessman confided in me that if he were to look at himself or other Christians for evidence of God he might have become discouraged and never known God. But because he focuses his attention on God, his relationship with his maker is vigorous and real. The concept of human frailty must never become a cop-out for sin. Gossip, pride, sexual sins, cheating, hate—all of these are not frailties but sins and, as such, roadblocks between the non-Christian and God. Lewis would be among the first to agree with this. Although he was not accepting of sin, he was a man of great brilliance and much humanness.

The Imperfection of Loneliness

A man of contrasts, C.S. Lewis was without a doubt one of the great intellectuals of the twentieth century. Yet in his letters he often wrote about simple things—his cats, his seemingly endless illnesses, and some of his homely answers for those illnesses. He shocked *Time* magazine by stating that he did indeed enjoy monotony. He admitted his deep fear of poverty; yet after his death it became known that he had been giving away two-thirds of his income. He hated solitude; and perhaps partly because of that he endured the presence of an increasingly irascible housekeeper, Mrs. Moore, for years until her death. He preferred the problems of an incompatible living partner over those of solitude.

He had his routines, his after-dinner glass of port and his evenings with Tolkien when each read the other's manuscripts. Yet he could be spontaneous, as in his last travels with Joy just months before her death.

Lewis's awareness of his aloneness in this world came early as a child when he learned of his mother's death. It was the beginning of his facing, when he was still a child, his impending adultness. In his words:

> "With my mother's death all settled happiness, all that was tranquil and reliable, disappeared from my life. There was to be much fun, many pleasures, many stabs of joy; but no more of the old security. It was sea and islands now; the great continent had sunk like Atlantis."[9]

Lewis never accepted his aloneness with feelings of comfortableness. Thus his fears, his closeness to his brother, his tolerance of Mrs. Moore, and his ecstasy and then deep sense of loss over his wife of three years are all understandable.

It is this combination of greatness and humanness in Lewis which is so encouraging to those of us who at times denigrate ourselves for being human.

Perspective on Human Value

Lewis had a gut respect for so-called ordinary people. In speaking of the "average" man Lewis commented:

> "It seems that there is a general rule in the moral universe which may be formulated 'The higher, the more in danger.' The 'average sensual man' who is sometimes unfaithful to his wife, sometimes tipsy, always a little selfish, now and then (within the law) a trifle sharp in his deals, is certainly, by ordinary standards, a 'lower' type than the man whose soul is filled with some great Cause, to which he will subordinate his appetites, his fortune, and even his safety. But it is out of the second man that something really fiendish can be made; an Inquisitor, a Member of the Committee of Public Safety. It is great men, potential saints, not little men, who become merciless fanatics. Those who are readiest to die for a cause may easily become those who are readiest to kill for it."[10]

Placing each person's value in proper perspective, as dependent upon God for real value, Lewis further explained:

> "Starting with the doctrine that every individuality is of infinite value, we picture God as a kind of employment committee whose business it is to find suitable careers for souls, square holes for square pegs. In fact, however, the value of the individual does not lie in himself. He is capable of receiving value. He receives it by union with Christ. There is no question of finding for him a place in the living temple which will do justice to his inherent value and give scope to his natural idiosyncrasy. The place was there first. The man was created for it. He will not be himself till he is there. We shall be true and everlasting and really divine persons only in Heaven, just as we are, even now, coloured bodies only in the light."[11]

It was not that Lewis either glorified or denigrated any status of man. He simply saw the imperfection involved in all levels of mankind and realized that man's true potential for good lay only in his relationship with God.

As an extension of that thought, Lewis believed that we are indeed our brother's keeper. As he put it, "There are no ordinary people." We are special to God and each other with sacred spiritual potential.

"Thus," says Lewis, "the load, or weight, or burden of my neighbour's glory should be laid daily on my back, a load so heavy that only humility can carry it, and the backs of the proud will be broken. It is a serious thing to live in a society of possible gods and goddesses, to remember that the dullest and most uninteresting person you talk to may one day be a creature which, if you saw it now, you would be strongly tempted to worship, or else a horror and corruption such as you now meet, if at all, only in a nightmare. All day long we are, in some degree, helping each other to one or other of these destinations. It is in the light of these overwhelming possibilities, it is with the awe and the circumspection proper to them, that we should conduct all our dealings with one another, all friendships, all loves, all play, all politics. There are no ordinary people. You have never talked to a mere mortal. Nations, cultures, arts, civilizations—these are mortal, and their life is to ours as the life of a gnat. But it is immortals whom we joke with, work with, marry, snub, and exploit—immortal horrors or everlasting splendours. This does not mean that we are to be perpetually solemn. We must play. But our merriment must be of that kind (and it is, in fact, the merriest kind) which exists between people who have, from the outset, taken each other seriously—no flippancy, no superiority, no presumption. And our charity must be a real and costly love, with deep feeling for the sins in spite of which we love the sinner—no mere tolerance or indulgence which parodies love as flippancy parodies merriment. Next to the Blessed Sacrament itself, your neighbour is the holiest object presented to your senses. If he is your Christian neighbour he is holy in almost the same way, for in him also Christ vere latitat—the glorifier and the glorified, Glory himself, is truly hidden."[12]

Were we to translate this viewpoint into actions in each of our lives, perhaps there would be little need for psychotherapists. Not, by the way, because needing therapy or counseling is sinful, but because loving our neighbor with all his imperfection, and his loving me back with all of mine, would be a good insurance policy against some of the problems which cause people to seek professional help.

Deceptive Reality

Imperfection can, at times, be deceptive, however. In spiritual matters our perception sometimes seems inadequate when compared to all that we perceive in the natural realm because we are so used to the natural. In our humanness we confuse reality with fiction, perfection with imperfection. Lewis gave an apt example:

"When I was a boy, gramophone records were not nearly so good as they are now. In the old recording of an orchestral piece you could hardly hear the separate instrument at all, but only a single undifferentiated sound. That was the sort of music I grew up on. And when, at a somewhat later age, I began to hear real orchestras, I was actually disappointed with them, just because you didn't get that single sound. What one got in a concert room seemed to me to lack the unity I had grown to expect, to be not an orchestra but merely a number of individual musicians on the same platform. In fact, I felt it 'wasn't the Real Thing.' This is an even better example than the former one. For a gramophone record is precisely a substitute, and an orchestra the reality. But owing to my musical miseducation the reality appeared to be a substitute and the substitute a reality."

Philosophically, Lewis explained his example:

"Things do look so very much as if our whole faith were a substitute for the real well-being we have failed to achieve on earth. It seems so very likely that our rejection of the World is only the disappointed fox's attempt to convince himself that unattainable grapes are sour. After all, we do not usually think much about the next world till our hopes in this have been pretty well flattened out—and when they are revived we not infrequently abandon our religion. And does not all that talk of celestial love come chiefly from monks and nuns, starved celibates consoling themselves with a compensatory hallucination? And the worship of the Christ child—does it not also come to us from centuries of lonely old maids? There is no good ignoring these disquieting thoughts. Let us admit from the outset that the psychologists have a good *prima facie* case. The theory that our religion is a substitute has a great deal of plausibility.

"Faced with this, the first thing I do is to try to find out what I know about substitutes, and the realities for which they are substituted, in general. And I find that I don't know so much as I thought I did. Until I considered the matter I had a sort of impression that one could recognize the difference by mere inspection if one was really honest—that the substitute would somehow betray itself by the mere taste, would ring false. And this impression was, in fact, one of the sources from which the doubts I mentioned were drawing their strength. What made it seem so likely that religion was a substitute was not any general philosophical argument about the existence of God, but rather the experienced fact that for the most of us at most times the spiritual life tasted so thin, or insipid, compared with the natural. And I thought that was just what a substitute might be expected to taste like. But after reflection, I discovered that this was not only not an obvious truth but was even contradicted by some of my own experience."[13]

Not long ago I experienced vividly this feeling of blurring—the real with the unreal—as I watched a play written by psychiatrist Viktor E. Frankl. Dr. Frankl had written this play shortly after his release from some of the worst Nazi concentration camps. It spoke movingly of the idea that life at all levels has meaning—even at the level of deep suffering. Meaning is the real substance of life. It is what makes life something more than superficial survival. As I sat in the audience I was moved by the reality of what I was seeing on stage. Truly the audience at that point was less real than the players. For the players were presenting life at its peak of meaning.

Related to this same idea that we do not always precisely identify reality, Lewis further explained how mere moods and simple circumstances often affect our spiritual beliefs and outlook:

"It is always assumed that the difficulties of faith are intellectual difficulties, that a man who has once accepted a certain proposition will automatically go on believing it till real grounds for disbelief occur. Nothing could be more superficial. How many of the freshmen who come up to Oxford from religious homes and lose their Christianity in the first year have been honestly *argued* out of it? How many of our own sudden temporary losses of faith have rational basis which would stand examination for a moment? I don't know how it is with others, but I find that mere change of scene always has a tendency to decrease my faith at first—God is less credible when I pray in a hotel bedroom than when I am in College. The society of unbelievers makes Faith harder even when they are people whose opinions, on any other subject, are known to be worthless.

"These irrational fluctuations in belief are not particular to religious belief. They are happening about all our beliefs all day long. Haven't you noticed it with our thoughts about the war? Some days, of course, there is really good or really bad news, which gives us rational grounds for increased optimism or pessimism. But everyone must have experienced days in which we are caught up in a great wave of confidence or down into a trough of anxiety

plans somewhat lightly and works from moment to moment 'as to the Lord.' It is only our daily bread that we are encouraged to ask for. The present is the only time in which any duty can be done or any grace received."[18]

I read these comforting words and felt better about my own less-than-perfect planning. I, too, am learning that "happy work is best done by the man who takes his long-term plans somewhat lightly and works from moment to moment 'as to the Lord.'"

Routine Prayer

In the matter of prayer Lewis wrote a comment in a letter that should relax any Christian who demands a certain routine experience in his or her daily prayer life:

"We all go through periods of dryness in our prayers, don't we? I doubt…whether they are necessarily a bad symptom. I sometimes suspect that what we *feel* to be our best prayers are really our worst; that what we are enjoying is the satisfaction of apparent success, as in executing a dance or reciting a poem. Do our prayers sometimes go wrong because we insist on trying to talk to God when he wants to talk to us?

"Joy tells me that once, years ago, she was haunted one morning by a feeling that God wanted something of her, a persistent pressure like the nag of a neglected duty. And till midmorning she kept on wondering what it was. But the moment she stopped worrying, the answer came through as plain as a spoken voice. It was 'I don't want you to *do* anything. I want to *give you* something' and immediately her heart was full of peace and delight.

"St. Augustine says, 'God gives where he finds empty hands.' A man whose hands are full of parcels can't receive a gift. Perhaps these parcels are not always sins or earthly cares, but sometimes our own fussy attempts to worship him in *our* way. Incidentally, what most often interrupts my own prayers is not great distractions but tiny ones—things one will have to do or avoid in the course of the next hour."[19]

Hang-ups and Moral Choices

Regarding psychological hang-ups Lewis was accepting of the very least up to the more severe. In his *Letters to an American Lady* he referred to her impending surgery with the words: "Fear is horrid but there's no reason to be ashamed of it. Our Lord was afraid (dreadfully so) in Gethsemane. I always cling to that as a very comforting fact." And that, in essence, is the very heart of C.S. Lewis and imperfection. He was much comforted by his Lord in the midst of the vicissitudes of life. God was not a club or a weapon to use against others. Lewis reverenced and feared him. Lewis knew his God too well to feel that he would not yet comfort his children who try so terribly hard at times to be perfect, and yet fail.

Perhaps in *Mere Christianity* Lewis expressed one of his clearest thoughts on psychological problems:

"When a man makes a moral choice two things are involved. One is the act of choosing. The other is the various feelings, impulses, and so on, which his psychological outfit presents him with, and which are the raw material of his choice. Now this raw material may be of two kinds. Either it may be what we would call normal: it may consist of the sort of feelings that are common to all men. Or else it may consist of quite unnatural feelings due to things that have gone wrong in his subconscious. Thus fear of things that are really dangerous would be an example of the first kind; an irrational fear of cats or spiders would be an example of the second kind. The desire of a man for a woman would be of the first kind; the perverted desire of a man for a man would be of the second. Now what psychoanalysis undertakes to do is to remove the abnormal feelings, that is, to give the man better raw material for his acts of choice. Morality is concerned with the acts of choice themselves.

"Put it this way. Imagine three men who go to war. One has the ordinary natural fear of danger that any man has and he subdues it by moral effort and becomes a brave man. Let us suppose that the other two have, as a result of things in their subconscious, exaggerated, irrational fears, which no amount of moral effort can do anything about. Now suppose that a psychoanalyst comes along and cures these two: that is, he puts them both back in the position of the first man. Well it is just then that the psychoanalytical problem is over and the moral problem begins. Because, now that they are cured, these two men might take quite different lines. The first might say, 'Thank goodness I've got rid of all those doo-dahs. Now at last I can do what I always wanted to do—my duty to the cause of freedom.' But the other might say, 'Well, I'm very glad that I now feel moderately cool under fire, but, of course, that doesn't alter the fact that I'm still jolly well determined to look after Number One and let the other chap do the dangerous job whenever I can. Indeed one of the good things about feeling less frightened is that I can now look after myself much more effficiently and can be much cleverer at hiding the fact from the others.' Now this difference is a purely moral one and psychoanalysis cannot do anything about it. However much you improve the man's raw material, you have still got something else: the real, free choice of the man, on the material presented to him, either to put his own advantage first or to put it last. And this free choice is the only thing that morality is concerned with.

"The bad psychological material is not a sin but a disease. It does not need to be repented of, but to be cured. And by the way, that is very important. Human beings judge one another by their external actions. God judges them by their moral choices. When a neurotic who has a pathological horror of cats forces himself to pick up a cat for some good reason, it is quite possible that in God's eyes he has shown more courage than a healthy man may have shown in winning the V.C. [Victoria Cross]. When a man who has been perverted from his youth and taught that cruelty is the right thing, does some tiny little kindness, or refrains from some cruelty he might have committed, and thereby, perhaps, risks being sneered at by his companions, he may, in God's eyes, be doing more than you and I would do if we gave up life itself for a friend.

"It is well to put this the other way round. Some of us who seem quite nice people may, in fact, have made so little use of a good heredity and a good upbringing that we are really worse than those whom we regard as fiends. Can we be certain how we should have behaved if we had been saddled with the psychological outfit, and then with the bad upbringing, and then with the power, say, of Himmler? That is why Christians are told not to judge. We see only the results which a man's choices make out of his raw material. But God does not judge him on the raw material at all, but on what he has done with it. Most of the man's psychological make-up is probably due to his body. When his body dies all that will fall off him, and the real central man, the thing that chose, that made the best or the worst out of this material, will stand naked. All sorts of nice things which we thought our own, but which were really due to a good digestion, will fall off some of us: all sorts of nasty things which were due to complexes or bad health will fall off others. We shall then, for the first time, see every one as he really was. There will be surprises."[20]

Learning to Love the "Others"

In the areas vital to Christian living, Lewis was not only practical but reassuring. How often we try to love and end up failing. To love those I find unlovable, I have discovered that I need to very honestly pray: "Lord, I

don't love _____, but I am willing to have you love _____
through me." Then I have learned, I must follow through by acting in love.
Similarly Lewis said:

"But though natural likings should normally be encouraged, it would be
quite wrong to think that the way to become charitable is to sit trying to
manufacture affectionate feelings. Some people are 'cold' by temperament;
that may be a misfortune for them, but it is no more a sin than having a
bad digestion is a sin; and it does not cut them out from the chance, or
excuse them from the duty, of learning charity. The rule for all of us is perfectly simple. Do not waste time bothering whether you 'love' your neighbour; act as if you did. As soon as we do this we find one of the great secrets.
When you are behaving as if you loved someone, you will presently come to
love him. If you injure someone you dislike, you will find yourself disliking
him more. If you do him a good turn, you will find yourself disliking him
less. There is, indeed, one exception. If you do him a good turn, not to
please God and obey the law of charity, but to show him what a fine for-
giving chap you are, and to put him in your debt, and then sit down to
wait for his 'gratitude,' you will probably be disappointed. (People are not
fools: they have a very quick eye for anything like showing off, or patronage.)
But whenever we do good to another self, just because it is a self, made
(like us) by God, and desiring its own happiness as we desire ours, we shall
have learned to love it a little more or, at least, to dislike it less."[21]

Struggling with Impropriety

In the area of chastity or modesty, Lewis speaks with refreshing candor
and balance. According to Lewis:

"The Christian rule of chastity must not be confused with the social rule
of 'modesty' (in one sense of that word); i.e. propriety, or decency. The social
rule of propriety lays down how much of the human body should be dis-
played and what subjects can be referred to, and in what words, according
to the customs of a given social circle. Thus, while the rule of chastity is
the same for all Christians at all times, the rule of propriety changes. A girl
in the Pacific islands wearing hardly any clothes and a Victorian lady completely covered in clothes might both be equally 'modest,' proper, or decent,
according to the standards of their own societies; and both, for all we could
tell by their dress, might be equally chaste (or equally unchaste). Some of the
language which chaste women used in Shakespeare's time would have been
used in the nineteenth century only by a woman completely abandoned.

When people break the rule of propriety current in their own time and place, if they do so in order to excite lust in themselves or others, then they are offending against chastity. But if they break it through ignorance or carelessness they are guilty only of bad manners. When, as often happens, they break it defiantly in order to shock or embarrass others, they are not necessarily being unchaste, but they are being uncharitable; for it is uncharitable to take pleasure in making other people uncomfortable. I do not think that a very strict or fussy standard of propriety is any proof of chastity or any help to it, and I therefore regard the great relaxation and simplifying of the rule which has taken place in my own lifetime as a good thing. At its present stage, however, it has this inconvenience, that people of different ages and different types do not all acknowledge the same standard, and we hardly know where we are. While this confusion lasts I think that old, or old-fashioned, people should be very careful not to assume that young or 'emancipated' people are corrupt whenever they are (by the old standard) improper; and, in return, that young people should not call their elders prudes or puritans because they do not easily adopt the new standard."22

Lewis concluded with the line which, while not compromising with sin, sets the stage for real acceptance of other people with their, at times, varying standards; "A real desire to believe all the good you can of others and to make others as comfortable as you can will solve most of the problems."

As a little girl I was not allowed to attend the theater. I can still remember receiving my parents' reluctant permission at times to see a Walt Disney movie. But I only half enjoyed it. I sat nervously near the aisle and watched the lights over the exit doors on either side of the theater. As long as they were still burning I knew God had not come and taken his own away, leaving me. The conditioning was deep, for until a few years ago theaters still made me edgy.

While some movies are sinful because of what they portray, I'm sure that my childhood was not corrupted by Walt Disney. Indeed the fantasy and, at times, pathos of those stories enriched those years. And in the whole area of ethics, that which is not directly sinful must be relegated to the individual conscience of the believer, which leaves room for imperfection to creep in. For example, there is the matter of temperance—how much TV we watch or how many movies we see, if we can find that many good ones! These are things we must work out. But "God knows our situation; he will not judge us as if we had no difficulties to overcome. What matters is the sincerity and perseverance of our will to overcome them."[23] If God does not judge, then neither should we judge ourselves or anyone else for imperfection.

I frequently counsel people who come from good Christian backgrounds and have turned against God because people in the church judged them where God would not have. Or, they were rightly judged, but without love.

Someday we who are Christians will have to give a reason for those so turned away. And in the same way others will have to account for the hurt they caused their brother who didn't turn away but who suffered under their intolerance. In the meantime, we who know our own imperfection can be more accepting of ourselves and of others because of God's love and acceptance of us. For God has perfect balance in contrast to our lack of it.

En route to Perfection

In the words of C.S. Lewis: "On the one hand, God's demand for perfection need not discourage you in the least in your present attempts to be good, or even in your present failures. Each time you fall he will pick you up again. And he knows perfectly well that your own efforts are never going to bring you anywhere near perfection. On the other hand, you must realise from the outset that the goal towards which he is beginning to guide you is absolute perfection; and no power in the whole universe, except you yourself, can prevent him from taking you to the goal."[24]

Continued Lewis: "When a man turns to Christ and seems to be getting on pretty well (in the sense that some of his bad habits are now corrected), he often feels that it would be natural if things went fairly smoothly. When troubles come along—illness, money troubles, new kinds of temptation—he is disappointed. These things, he feels, might have been necessary to rouse him and make him repent in his bad old days; but why now? Because God is forcing him on, or up, to a higher level: putting him into situations where he will have to be very much braver, or more patient, or more loving, than he ever dreamed of being before. It seems to us all unnecessary: but that is because we have not yet had the slightest notion of the tremendous thing he means to make of us.

"I find I must borrow yet another parable from George MacDonald. Imagine yourself as a living house. God comes in to rebuild that house. At first, perhaps, you can understand what he is doing. He is getting the drains right and stopping the leaks in the roof and so on: you knew that those jobs needed doing and so you are not surprised. But presently he starts knocking the house about in a way that hurts abominably and does not seem to make sense. What on earth is he up to? The explanation is that he is building quite a different house from the one you thought of—throwing out a new wing here, putting on an extra floor there, running up towers, making court-yards. You thought you were going to be made into a decent little cottage: but he is building a palace. He intends to come and live in it himself."25

In our own efforts we can be nothing but imperfect. As human beings, God still loves us, imperfect as we are. And, in the words of C.S. Lewis:

"If we let him—for we can prevent him, if we choose—he will make the feeblest and filthiest of us into a god or goddess, a dazzling, radiant, immor-tal creature, pulsating all through with such energy and joy and wisdom and love as we cannot now imagine, a bright stainless mirror which reflects back to God perfectly (though, of course, on a smaller scale) his own bound-less power and delight and goodness. The process will be long and in parts very painful; but that is what we are in for. Nothing less. He meant what he said."26

G. Campbell Morgan

G. Campbell Morgan was a British Preacher considered by some to be the Bible Expositor of his generation.

". . .Unbelief is the most irrational attitude possible to man. The man who attempts to account for the things in the midst of which he lives by the things in the midst of which he lives, is bereft of reason. I use the expression carefully; the rationality of faith. To me it is infinitely more difficult to believe in this world as I see it—I do not mean as man has often spoiled it, but as it is in itself—its mountains and valleys, its oceans and continents, its magnificent splendours, without a God, than with the God of the Bible accounting for it. I cannot believe that the God in Whom I am bound to believe, Who fashioned the daisy and made a man—I care nothing for the moment about the process—is careless about the man, and not interested in him. If I admit God has some care for human life in any way, I cannot believe He is careless about the highest thing in human life which is the moral element and capacity. Faith is utterly rational. To try and account for the things that are by the things that are is to work in a vicious circle. It is the man of faith, the man who endures as seeing Him Who is invisible—mark the contradiction and paradox, and face them—seeing Him Who is invisible, who is the man of rationality. That is the man of reason, that is the man of sanity; that is the man who is not mad."[1]

"...Why did the men of Antioch call these people Christians? There can be but one answer, a simple answer, and yet including the whole fact. They saw that these people had been with the Christ in spirit, if not in

190

(1863–1945)

actual personality, and that they had learned of Him. They talked of Christ, lived for Christ, worked for Christ. They had caught His Spirit, they were occupied with His business, and were manifesting Him in character and conduct; and the men of Antioch said, These people are Christians, men connected with Christ in some way."[2]

"A man never finds real freedom of the will until he has found the seat of authority, and has put Christ there as King. Christ knew that. That was His meaning, when He said, 'Seek ye first His Kingdom and His righteousness; and all these things shall be added unto you.'"[3]

"...So surely as the Christ life is in us, with merciless, ruthless, and pitiless determination our life will be poured out in unceasing attack upon the strongholds of evil in the city, in the nation, in the home, and everywhere. In the wilderness Jesus said, 'Get thee hence, Satan,' and He will never cease His work until the enemy is finally cast out. If our life be Christ's life, then we can never sign a truce with evil. We cannot sit down and be indifferent to its presence.

"...The Christ life was that of authority over evil. Because Christ has won the battle already, the life of His follower shares His authority. It is most interesting to notice in the study of the life of Jesus that from that wilderness temptation on to the end, He never argued with the devil again. Whenever He came into contact with him, or with the evil spirits, it was with the tone of authority, and the authority was immediately obeyed."[4]

191

CHAPTER 11

Ruth Bell Graham: Reference Points

A young girl darted out of an appliance store which she and several dozen other people were looting during the 1992 Los Angeles riots. Hesitating at the front of the store she seemed to be deciding which direction to choose in her escape. At that moment she was confronted by a reporter.

Looking at the armful of stolen goods, he questioned: "Isn't this stealing? Isn't it wrong?"

"I suppose so," she answered hesitantly. Then, as she looked around at her friends and then back at the reporter, her confidence was renewed. "Actually it must not be so wrong," she countered. "Look around you. Everyone is doing it."

This young girl had obviously been taught that stealing was wrong. Perhaps she had learned that from her family or her church. Now her reference point, that standard to which she referred to determine right and wrong, had shifted. Her new reference point of morality became "What is everyone around me doing?" Because the reference point changed, the behavior also changed.

A friend of mine who builds houses defined the term reference point as "a starting point for describing any piece of real estate." In her book *It's My Turn* Ruth Bell Graham, wife of evangelist Billy Graham, wrote a concise piece on the concept of reference points:

"There is a small bronze disk on the Meads' ranch in north central Kansas where the thirty-ninth parallel from the Atlantic to the Pacific crosses the ninety-eighth meridian running from Canada to the Rio Grande.

"The National Ocean Survey, a small federal agency whose business it is to locate the exact position of every point in the United States, uses the scientifically recognized reference point on the Meads' ranch. So far, no mistakes have been made, and none are expected.

"All ocean liners and commercial planes come under the survey. The government can build no dams or even shoot off a missile without this agency to tell it exact locations—to the very inch." [1]

To show what can happen if such a reference point is *not* used, Ruth Graham gives an apt example: "The State Highway Department in Pennsylvania once set out to build a bridge, working from both sides. When the workers reached the middle of the waterway, they found they were thirteen feet to one side of each other. Alfred Steinberg, writing some time ago in "The Saturday Evening Post," went on to explain that each crew of workmen had used its own reference point."[2] Like the girl looting during the riots, there was no central reference point. Each used their own reference point.

One is reminded of the verse in 11 Cor. 10:12: "For we dare not make ourselves of the number, or compare ourselves with some that commend themselves: but they measuring themselves by themselves, and comparing themselves among themselves, are not wise."

To Ruth Graham our reference point in the spiritual realm is "the Living Word and the Written Word... It's not a physical place. It's not a certain place in my room or house. It's the Living Word and the Written Word. And I think that's what's happening to our country. We've lost our reference point." Living in constant communion with that reference point she lives a day by day, moment by moment life of "total reliance upon the person of Jesus Christ," to use her daughter Gigi's terminology.

The Grahams' eldest daughter Gigi Graham Tchividjian bears living testimony to that day by day turning to the Divine Reference Point. Says Gigi, speaking of the hard times which her mother faced: "...All these years her immediate reaction has been to throw herself on the Lord and the Scriptures. As a child I can remember her leaving her Bible open in a prominent place, so she could just get a verse every now and then. We found her often by her bed, on her knees. She had her Bible anywhere she was in the house, sometimes even on the ironing board. There would be a verse that she would be gleaning and meditating upon." The result of the constant turning to her heavenly reference point? "Mother shared with us the sunshine; and she kept the tears and heartache and difficulties from us."

For Ruth, Christ as her reference point started when she was very young. Born of missionary parents in China, Ruth once said: "I can never recall going to sleep at night without hearing gunshots in the countryside around the house."[3] Walking to school, she passed daily by a place where, according to pagan custom, dead babies were thrown away. Another memory from childhood is watching a crowd laughing while they beat a mad dog to death. "It contrasted so with the kindness of the Christians I knew, and it made a deep impression."[4]

Of those early days, Ruth said to me: "I think God brought me up tough for a good reason and I'm grateful." In further explanation, she added: "I prayed early on for a tough hide and a tender heart." As a result of that training, when hurtful and controversial things are said about Billy Graham, her attitude is: "I know who he is and what he is, and what his motives are. And so nothing that anyone else can say about him would, in any way, make me think the less of him."

Yet, in spite of the hard training, her basic memory of that childhood in China remains one of "love, acceptance, and fun. Mother ran a tight ship," she said to me. "My mother and daddy both did; but it was a happy home. Lots of singing and lots of laughter and lots of love."

Citing Christmas as an example, she continued: "Christmas was Christmas like you have never seen it over here. We even had candles in the Christmas trees. We didn't have electric lights . . .I cannot imagine how they had live candles in the Christmas tree without burning the whole house down. But they just went out of their way to make it happy. Yet never once did Santa Claus eclipse Christ. We always knew that it was Jesus' birthday. We had the stockings and all that went with it, but it was Christ's birthday; and it was one of the happiest, happiest days of the whole year."

Reminiscent of Gigi's word about her mother, Ruth said of her own mother: "I think the greatest tribute to Mother's courage is that we children never sensed fear and we ourselves never had any fear."[5] Similarly, in her book *Prodigals and Those Who Love Them* she says: "We must take care, we parents, that we speak less of the problems, the difficulties, the headaches and heartaches and backaches in this work than we do of Him and His glory. Indeed, I question the wisdom of even mentioning the former when the children are small."[6]

Within Ruth Graham's personality is a deep sensitivity and seriousness, balanced by a well developed sense of humor. As a child her love for God was so great that at the end of each day she would kneel by her bed and pray that God would let her die for Him, a prayer that was quickly countered by her sister Rosa who prayed: "Please, God, don't listen to her."[7] By the time she reached her teens her single desire was to be a missionary in Tibet. Her dedication to the will of God is seen unmistakably in a poem she wrote before leaving China for College in the United States.

> Spare not the pain
> though the way I take
> be lonely and dark,
> though the whole soul ache,
> for the flesh must die
> though the heart may break.
> Spare not the pain, oh,
> spare not the pain.
> *Used by permission of author.*

In contrast to the dedicated, serious side of her personality, Ruth's sense of humor has been a great balancing factor in her life. Among her family and friends she is known for her practical jokes. On the day the young Billy Graham came to visit her, dressed in white from head to toe and carrying in his pocket a gold engagement ring, Ruth, unaware of his intentions, chose that day for a practical joke. With the help of a friend, she blacked out her front teeth, let her long hair hang loose, and put on a frumpy, flowered housedress, that was at least two sizes too big. Barefoot, she set off down the road to meet Billy.

Driving along the dusty road Billy stared at what he would later call the "snaggle-toothed" mountain girl, who also stared back at him. Finally recognizing her, he opened the car door numbly, and then began to laugh. Near dusk, at the top of a mountain, undaunted, he gave her the ring.[8]

The relationship had a humorous climax, but few marriages have had more serious impact on the world. To most of the world, Billy Graham is seen as having a more major impact on the twentieth century than almost any other human being. God has used him in a miraculous way. Yet behind the impact of the Billy Graham ministries has been the support and force of a very special woman of God. In 1942 Ruth wrote the words:

> Lord, common things
> are all I've ever asked
> of Thee.

But Ruth Bell Graham has lived a very uncommon life. The little girl who prayed to be a martyr, and the young woman who asked only for a common life, got neither. God said "No" to both prayers. What a blessing it is that God does not always say, "Yes." What God did give her, however, was a very real sense of how to follow Him in a day by day fashion, always referring back to His Word and His Person as her reference point.

At about the time Ruth Bell left China she wrote out what she wanted in a husband—in spite of the fact that she had decided to remain single and be a missionary!

> "If I marry:
> He must be so tall that when he is on his knees, as one has said, he reaches all the way to Heaven.
> His shoulders must be broad enough to bear the burden of a family.
> His lips must be strong enough to smile, firm enough to say no, and tender enough to kiss.
> Love must be so deep that it takes its stand in Christ and so wide that it takes the whole lost world in.
> He must be active enough to be gentle and great enough to be thoughtful.
> His arms must be strong enough to carry a little child. [9]
> *Used by permission of author.*

Later, but before they were married, Ruth wrote what seems to me to be her counterpart:

> God, make me worthy to be his wife:
> as cliffs are made, so make me strong,
> a help for him when things go wrong.
> Clear as the dew, Lord, make my mind,
> clear as the dew, and just as kind;
> and make me a refreshment too,

a quiet encourager, like You;
I'll laugh with him in face of tears,
In face of worries and of fears;
brave to be and do and bear,
both quick to yield, and glad to share.
Remind him, God, through coming days
how warm is my love for him always.
His head's held high as he faces life;
God, make me worthy to be his wife.
Used by permission of author.

The standards for both were high. But they were God's standards. Furthermore those standards have been possible to fulfill because there is a very practical, common sense element in their view of marriage.

In her book *It's My Turn,* Ruth gives a simple example of this common-sense, as well as some good advice for a successful marriage. One day when she stopped by the home of an elderly couple in their church, the husband said to Ruth: "'Would you like to know the secret of our happy marriage?' Of course I would.

"He led me into their study, where there stood two cluttered rolltop desks; I was surveying these with genuine interest when he explained, 'I never disturb her desk. And she never disturbs mine.'"

As a couple the Grahams balance each other in the area of temperament. Ruth is positive and Billy tends to worry. From the perspective of a daughter, Gigi sums up the differences between her parents succinctly when she says:

"...Daddy walks in the room and tension follows him. Mother walks into the room and peace follows her." Says Ruth more simply: "Some people are born worriers."

Both Gigi and her mother refer to Billy Graham as "Puddleglum," the Marsh-wiggle in *The Silver Chair* by C.S. Lewis. For those who have not read the *Chronicles of Narnia,* or who do not remember Puddleglum, a typical interchange between Puddleglum and his friends, as portrayed by Lewis, reads like this:

"'Good-by, dear Puddleglum,' said Jill going over to the Marsh-wiggle's bed. 'I'm sorry we called you a wet blanket.'

'So'm I,' said Eustace. 'You've been the best friend in the world.'

'And I do hope we'll meet again,' added Jill.

'Not much chance of that, I should say,' replied Puddleglum. 'I don't reckon I'm very likely to see my old wigwam again either. ...'"

With insight into the true character of Puddleglum, Jill concludes: "'Puddleglum! You're a regular old humbug. You sound as doleful as a funeral and I believe you're perfectly happy. And you talk as if you were afraid of everything, when you're really as brave as—as a lion.'"[11]

With similar optimism Ruth Graham concluded: "I'm married to a Puddleglum. And yet he turns out to be the most sterling character I've ever known."

In an amusing anecdote of her own Puddleglum, Ruth relates the following incident: "...we landed at the Miami airport. Bill had to stay, while I was to fly home. He checked the weather and learned it was not good in Atlanta, Georgia, where I would have to change planes for Asheville, North Carolina.

"'You probably won't be able to land,' he predicted. 'If not, I don't know where you will go—probably on to New York City. But if they try to land, I hope you make it; Atlanta is one of the busiest airports in the United States. And if you do, I'd advise you to spend the night in a motel—if you can get a room, which I doubt—as a lot of planes will be grounded and the motels will be full. In that case, rent a car, if you can get one, and drive home. But drive carefully because...'

"You guessed it. ...you could have a wreck.'"[12]

According to Gigi both of her parents are intense or high-strung in personality, but in different ways: "Mother's always thinking of something, always doing something. Sitting on a plane with her last Fall, my husband leaned over and said, "Gigi, look at your mother. You're just like her. She's always doing something. She's always writing notes or reading something."

Of her father's lifelong determination to live with eternity's values in view, Gigi said: "I have been with him and watched him change his mind about something. And it's not because he's just changing his mind. It's because his first reaction was, 'No, I can't do it.' Then he starts to think more about it. He begins to change because he realizes that from Eternity's point of view he might never have an opportunity to speak to this person again. I think Daddy really looks at things from Eternity's perspective...He always tries to remind us: 'How would you look at this from Eternity?'"

Because their reference point is Jesus Christ, their two lives, which are different in many ways, have blended together in a marriage which has lasted over the years. They have learned to enjoy their similarities and complement their differences. No one who talks to Ruth Graham for any length of time can fail to realize the depth of love that this very public but very private couple have for each other.

Whether it relates to differences of temperament in a marriage, or clinical depression, or prodigal children, or hormone imbalances, when Ruth Graham discusses emotional pain there is a delightful absence of the "Confess your Depression" mentality. Indeed, she sounds a great deal more like a favorite writer of hers, F. W. Boreham, when he says: "Humanity is a strange tangle; and no man can say where the work of the doctor ends and the work of the minister begins."[13]

It is also quite clear that she has suffered and that she understands the depth to which pain can go. She once wrote:

> Don't talk to me yet;
> the wound is fresh,
> the nauseous pain
> I can't forget
> fades into numbness
> like a wave,
> then comes again.
> Your tears I understand,
> But grief is deaf;
> It cannot hear the words
> you gently planned
> and tried to say.
> But . . .
> pray . . .
> *Used by permission of author.*

Yet characterisically she always goes on. In commenting on a prolonged bout of depression which she experienced during her pregnancy with her youngest child Ned, with positiveness she said: "I'm glad I had that, because it helps to understand how people feel. It was just nine months of a depression and then as soon as he was born it was over." Truly putting her Christian beliefs into shoeleather, she added: "Thank God that David wasn't always on a perpetual high. What would we do without the Psalms?"

So often we miss God's blessing when we are depressed or anxious because rather than seeking His comfort in the middle of the feelings we are busy blaming ourselves for being human. In a poem written in 1980, Ruth speaks of God's kindness in the *middle* of feelings of depression.

Sunk in this gray
depression
I cannot pray.
How can I give
expression
with no words
to say?
This mass of vague
foreboding
of aching care
love with its
overloading
short-circuits prayer,
Then in this fog
of tiredness
this nothingness, I find
a quiet, certain, knowing
that He is kind.
Used by permission of author.

It is difficult for me as a counselor to deal with some of the extreme views which are so frequently put forth by some Christians. For example, some who want God's reference point for morality, or purity, or holiness seem often to ignore His standard on love and compassion. Others who go to an opposite extreme speak of a cheap kind of love which demands little in the way of holiness.

Most people have difficulty understanding other people's pain, unless it is the kind of pain which they, too, have experienced. If I am depressed, for example, I will understand your depression better than your anxiety. Indeed I may be more willing to excuse your frailty, even your sin, if it is also my frailty or my sin.

For the Christian, while there are times when God allows us to suffer in a particular way so that we will better understand the problems of others, because of Christ in me, I can also take His compassion and understanding for that which I may *never* experience. Ruth Graham has done a remarkable job of combining high standards with deep compassion in the most difficult areas of life. The desire to do so started early and is reflected in a poem written from school in Korea in 1934.

"Inasmuch" a cup of water
offered one in Jesus' name,
"Inasmuch" a gentle handclasp
treating one and all the same,
"Inasmuch" a single penny
dropped in some poor beggar's palm,
"Inasmuch" a piece of clothing
just to keep a body warm,
"Inasmuch," so said the Master
(though the very least he be),
"Inasmuch as done to someone
you have done it unto me."
Used by permission of author.

Even when failure or sin is involved, while she has a high standard for Christian living, at the same time she has a higher standard than most for the necessity of acting in love and never giving up. She once said to a Sunday School class she was teaching: "When a person seems at his worst, we should demonstrate Jesus' love the most. When a child falls, you don't avoid or scold him, you help him up and comfort and encourage him."[14] That is what Christ did.

Similarly, with reference to prodigals, she speaks of unconditional love, the kind that is not earned but is freely given: "Prodigals need to know that they are loved at all times, and no matter what happens, that they are welcome home." In a personal reference she added: "We made it a point to keep the contact open to where they could make long-distance calls collect...God loves us unconditionally, and He allows us to call Him person to person and collect any time." Repeatedly there is that Divine Reference point. In this instance it is, loving, not as the world loves, but as God loves. Sometimes we look pretty good when we compare ourselves to others. But He is our Standard, not our friends or those whom we observe around us.

Furthermore, what other people think is not nearly so important as what happens to the prodigal or the one who is not prodigal at all, but, like David of old, is simply downcast. Gigi feels that her mother's poems more than her prose reveal her soul. Certainly that soul, and the souls of a great multitude of those who have prodigals, is revealed in the following poem.

They felt good eyes upon them
and shrank within—undone;
good parents had good children
and they—a wandering one.

The good folk never meant
to act smug or condemn,
but having prodigals
just "wasn't done" with them.

Remind them gently, Lord,
how You
have trouble with your children,
too.
Used by permission of author.

In putting her faith into shoeleather, Ruth can be very practical. When others might sermonize, she offers advice in short statements which are profound in their wisdom. In a conversation which revolved around prodigals and the frustration people feel in trying to make their children come back to the Lord, she commented: "Something that helped me tremendously was when it finally dawned on me that *we* take care of the possible and trust *God* for the impossible." Speaking of someone who had sought her advice, she added: "I had the feeling that this poor woman was tyring to do God's work for Him instead of her own. I think sometimes we do that. We just wade around trying to do the impossible."

After I wrote these words yesterday, I spent some time with two young people about whom I care a great deal. We talked about their struggles, and I longed to see them happy in their new-found relationship. Then I realized I was trying to do it for them. I thought of that word "impossible" and realized that I was trying to do the impossible. None of us can get into the life of another and make the problems go away. Even if we could, none of us have the time and energy to live our own life and even one other. We can listen; we can advise. But *they* must make the changes. And God in them must be the motivation and the power for such changes. That does not mean that the situation which I encountered is impossible for God. Simply, it means that I have done what I can to help. I have done the possible. Now I must leave the impossible to Him.

Parenting is an area where Ruth Graham offers advice which is sound and yet realistic. Many Christians sneer at the notion of quality time given to children by parents who work. These people assume that any mother who works out of the home wants to abdicate her parental role and just make more money. There are such parents, it is true. But most mothers want to raise their own children.

Says Ruth: "I think children are wise enough to know when a parent is working because they want a second car or a finer home or more things, or when they're working because they absolutely have to to keep bread on the table…They'll understand whether their parents put them first or possessions first…" With reassurance to those who feel continually guilty because they literally don't have enough time to spend with their children, she adds: "I think it's not the quantity of time you spend with your child. It's the quality of it…Close, loving companionship: they'll remember that rather than a whole day of indifference."

Her practical wisdom does not end when the issues become heavy and controversial. For is not God the God of the impossible? I once shared my concern over a young man who had refused to accept Christ as Saviour and then in a drunken stupor drove his motorcycle into a pole and died. In speaking of the Godly parents who were distraught, I asked: "What would you say to them?" She answered honestly, "I don't know." But then added something which I found to be of great help. "I remember a little couplet I heard somewhere. I do not know where it came from. I do not know who wrote it. But it said: 'Between the saddle and the ground, mercy I sought and mercy found.'" Then with conviction she added: "So many parents don't live to see their prayers answered. But I'm convinced God will answer our prayers…We don't know what happens in that last split second…I really think that we cannot begin to comprehend the mercy of God."

Of the suicide of a young man she was realistic about the family: "They'll go through it, but they'll never get over it." Yet when confronted with those who say that Christians who kill themselves will go to Hell, her response was immediate: "That's baloney! God knows when a person is pushed beyond endurance. And I love this saying: 'God did not call him home, but God welcomed him.'" When I shared that with a patient not long ago, visible waves of relief swept over his face and he was comforted.

Death faced in God's timing is not always easy, even for the Christian. Many years ago I remember hearing J. Sidlow Baxter say that he didn't fear death itself but he certainly didn't look forward to the process. His realism comforted me more than if he had promised that for the Christian the process is pure joy. It's not always so; we all know that. And to think that somehow we must make it a happy time in order to honor God makes it even harder. A poem written in 1974 expresses this thought well and balances the two extremes of abject fear and the attitude that somehow death must be pleasant to honor God.

"Death, be not long.
Death, be not hard,"
we prayed.
But days stretched year-like
and when death came, God
it was not made
easy as we had prayed.
Quiet, but not easy.

Forgive all my complaints;
for precious to You
is the death of Your saints.
Used by permission of author.

Unknown to most, Ruth Graham's practical wisdom extends way beyond words. She is a doer, and no task is too menial for her to perform. The cup of cold water is quite literal. On a simple level, when I expressed an interest in reading an author which is a favorite of hers but is hard to find, I planned to start a search in old book stores. To my surprise a few days later three of the man's books arrived in the mail, mailed in haste while she was rushing to get away on a trip. Such an act is typical of her thoughtfulness and generosity.

But the cup of cold water extends far beyond a simple act of kindness to actions which go back to Christ's example on this earth and our Lord's teaching. A man named Arthur Radcliffe who taught horticulture in North Carolina later managed a flower shop and was an usher in the Montreat Presbyterian Church. Around the time Ruth started teaching her Sunday School class, the man was placed in a nursing home in Greensboro, North Carolina. Radcliffe was now in his seventies.

Miserable in his separation from the plants and soil he loved to work with, he ran away and landed at Ruth's door. "'I'm not going to let the highway patrol take me back!' he declared, his voice rising. 'I'll die before I'll go back to that nursing home.' Then he begged, his eyes gleaming. 'Why don't you just let me die right here in this old cabin you got at the end of the road?'"[15]

Ruth fixed up the cabin and Radcliffe moved in. Two years later he died after having worked his beloved earth once again.

At times poor families have had their houses fixed, food provided, clothing given. Yet always the dignity of the individual involved is preserved. Their permission is asked rather than having help forced upon them.

In one situation, after asking an ill father if he would accept help, Ruth found out the sizes of all his children. Then on Christmas Eve she sent her husband and the children down the mountain to deliver clothes, along with some toys. Later, when the man was being ignored in the hospital, in spite of being in pain and having difficulty breathing, Ruth put in a call which made the place buzz with activity. The man ended up with the immediate care of a private nurse and a doctor. Dying, he whispered: "I want you to see that all my debts is paid. And I want my children raised as Christians."[16] To that man it was quite clear that all this love went back to a very personal relationship with Jesus Christ, a relationship he wanted for his children.

One of Ruth Graham's most touching poems relates back to a relationship with a woman in London which has extended over the years to this day. A characteristic of our Lord is that, while He is always a Gentleman and doesn't intrude and force Himself upon people, He doesn't give up on people either. In that way, too, He is our reference point.

Ruth first met Meg during a crusade in England. Meg had a drug problem, and through the years went through other problems ranging from lesbianism to promiscuity and pregnancy. Ruth has prayed for Meg, met her in coffee shops when she has been in England, and encouraged her in letters.

Early in their relationship Meg sadly commented: "I wish I had a mother like you."[17] Ruth is probably the closest Meg has come to being mothered.

On the plane after a seemingly futile encounter with Meg, Ruth wrote:

Perhaps
she will land
upon that Shore,
not in full sail,
but rather
a bit of broken wreckage
for Him
to gather.

Perhaps
He walks those Shores
seeking such

who have believed
a little
suffered much
and so
have been washed Ashore.

Perhaps
of all the souls redeemed
they most adore.
Used by permission of author.

The end result of finding our reference point in the Person of Jesus Christ is that those around us see Christ living through us. Gigi said of her mother: "When we went through the hard times, the first thing we saw her do was grab a Bible." That private reference point has issued forth into a public example that Christianity really does work.

Gigi told me of a time when her mother was visiting her in Paris, France, while Billy Graham was in some other part of the world. A family crisis arose which was disturbing and needed attending to. Gigi had already planned a dinner party with some friends whom her mother had not met. Yet when Gigi offered to cancel the dinner, feeling that the stress on her mother would be too great, Ruth told her "No." When the guests arrived, in Gigi's words, "We just had a good time and they left."

Months later the friends told Gigi that the impression "that came from your mother that night and that just stayed with us was her peace…" She had turned to her Reference Point and found her way.

In a related way Ruth told me how when one of her sons was going through a period of rebellion he worked in an office situation where a younger man treated an older man with rudeness and unfairness. Yet the older man was a saint in his behavior. He never retaliated; he never answered back. "He was just his sweet, gracious Christian self. He had no idea…of the effect his actions were having on the seventeen year old prodigal who was quietly watching." She concluded: "…God lets us be treated rudely, unpleasantly, or have difficult things happen to us from time to time so that the world can see how we react to them." What we show to the world by how we react to suffering becomes part of the specific meaning of our own individual suffering. How to find that meaning in the first place is by continually finding our reference point in Jesus Christ.

A statement which is characteristic of Ruth Bell Graham, and one which she seems to refer to frequently, is "Make the least of all that goes and the most of all that comes. And keep looking forward. Don't look backwards." The statement reflects a contentment which is only found in those who in Augustinian terms have found their repose in Him. It reflects a cup half full attitude rather than a cup half empty.

The Grahams live in a place they have called Little Piney Cove in a log cabin in the mountains of North Carolina. "When retired heavyweight boxer Muhammad Ali visited in the fall of 1979," he said to the press: "I thought he lived on a thousand acre farm...And we drove up to this house made of logs; [it was] the kind of house a man of God would live in."[18] (He graciously refused Billy's invitation to spend the night there.)

In the fall of 1975 Ruth wrote:

> We bought this cove
> when coves were cheap,
> and flatland scarce,
> and mountains steep.
> But not once
> were we told
> That here, in autumn
> all the poplars
> turn to gold.
>
> Oh, it was cheap
> (beyond belief)
> but autumn makes me feel
> a thief.
> *Used by permission of author.*

In contrast, right after the Grahams were married, Billy Graham took a pastorate outside of Wheaton, Illinois, without talking about it to his new bride. He not only accepted the pastorate, but also choose the apartment without consulting her. As Gigi said: "When she got there she found this dreary, dingy, horrible little apartment. But she made do the best she could." Then she found some red fabric and fixed it on the wall with a light shining on it so that "she could pretend it was a fireplace on dreary nights...and she could sit with a cup of tea or coffee..."

According to Ruth "it was a piece of bright, red Chinese embroidery...and I hung it on the wall and had a floor lamp that I shined on it to give it an illusion of a fireplace because I didn't have one. I just love a fireplace in cold weather," she added. "It's pretty. It's company."

To quote once again from Frank Boreham: "There is a magic that turns prisons into palaces and crusts into dainties. There is a wonder that wraps a man about, and thenceforth no humiliation can degrade him, no banishment can exile him, no poverty can make him poor, and no death can destroy him."[19]

To make the best of what is has been a life-long pattern for Ruth. Explained Gigi: "She never complained. As soon as Daddy walked out the door, with tears in her eyes she would turn around and say: 'Okay, let's prepare for his homecoming.' And we would turn around and do a project: cleaning the attic, building a treehouse, or whatever."

"Make the least of all that goes and the most of all that comes" does not result in the eradication of pain in this life, but it does lead to contentment. For Ruth Bell Graham life always goes on. But underneath that going on, there is a constant referral to the Person of Jesus Christ, a constant taking of time to "indulge herself in the Lord."[20] Perhaps it is impossible to be anything but content when you walk moment by moment, hand in hand, with the King of Kings.

"Therefore, indeed, Seeing that we also have encircling us so great a cloud of witnesses, Stripping off every incumbrance and the easily entangling sin, With endurance let us be running the race that is lying before us."[1]

Joseph Bryant Rotherham

"Are we to think of all these as spectators in an amphitheatre looking down upon those who were contestants in the arena below? It seems to me it is not so easy to decide this question as some have thought. Our English word 'witness' can be used in two very distinct senses. It may mean to behold, or on the other hand simply to bear testimony. It would seem as though the original word here used has distinctly the latter sense, so that those of whom we have read in Chapter 11 are really testimony-bearers to the power of faith. On the other hand, the apostle clearly seems to indicate that there is a sense in which we are surrounded by a great cloud of spectators who apparently are looking down upon us, while themselves witnessing to the grandeur of faith. But in any case, it is intended to be a message of encouragement to those who are still in the place of testing."[2]

H.A. Ironside

If Only
Hebrews 12:1

"Compassed about
with a great cloud..."

210

the Scriptures say;
If only I could hear,
one shout, the distant roar
of that great crowd,
just some small word
aloud...
aloud...
to cheer my way.[3]

Ruth Bell Graham
Minneapolis, October 22, 1980

"'We have, lying around us, so great a cloud of witnesses' (ver. 1). 'We' are running, like the competitors in the Hellenic stadium, in the public view of a mighty concourse, so vast, so aggregated, so placed aloft, that no word less great than 'cloud' occurs as its designation:...True, the multitudinous watchers are unseen, but this only gives faith another opportunity of exercise; we are to treat the Blessed as seen, for we know that they are there, living to God, one with us, fellows of our life and love. So let us address ourselves afresh to the spiritual race, the course of faith...

"I thus explain the 'witnesses' to mean spectators, watchers, not testifiers. The context seems to me to decide somewhat positively for this explanation. It is an altogether pictorial context; the imagery of the foot-race comes suddenly up, and in a moment raises before us the vision of the stadium and its surroundings. The reader cannot see the course with his inner eyes without also seeing those hosts of eager lookers-on which made, on every such occasion, in the old world as now, the life of the hour. In such a context nothing but explicit and positive reasons to the contrary could give to the word 'witnesses,' and to the word 'cloud' in connection with it, any other allusion. True, these watchers are all, as a fact, evidential 'witnesses' also, testifiers to the infinite benefit and success of the race of faith. But that thought lies almost hidden behind the other. It is as loving, sympathetic, inspiring lookers-on that the old saints, from Abel onwards, are here seen gathered, thronging and intent, around us as we run.

" . . . We ask, and ask in vain, what is the medium through which these observers watch us, the air and light, as it were, in which their vision acts; what is their proximity to us all the while; to what extent they are able to know the entire conditions of our race. But all this leaves faith in peaceful possession of a fact of unspeakable animation. It tells the discouraged or tired Christian, tempted to think of the unseen as a dark void, that it is rather a bright and populous world, in mysterious touch and continuity with this, and that our forerunners, from those of the remotest past down to the last-called beloved one who has passed out of our sight, know enough about us to mark our advance and to prepare their welcome at the goal."[4]

Handley C.G. Moule

CHAPTER 12

Living Within an Eternal Perspective

I t was in Mexico that I realized most fully—and for the first time in my life—that a whole host of situations in life cannot be eradicated. As a child, for example, going to a doctor meant to me that one would be automatically well. Then a little friend of mine died from polio, even though her father was a doctor. When I was in my teens I was hurt in an automobile accident. As I waited for the ambulance, I remember a kind man bending down saying, "We never think that this can happen to us." And I didn't think it could. But it did. And I kept having flash thoughts that this had to be just a nightmare and I would soon wake up.

Yet throughout my early life I held on tenaciously to the notion that a problem could always be conquered, eliminated, done away with. Injustice could be abolished if we worked hard enough. The impossible just took a little longer, as the saying goes. Disillusionment came at times when my theory failed, but I rationalized that with a little more work the next attempt would be successful.

Somehow in Mexico the beginning of realism broke through upon my thinking. It's not that I became less idealistic. For more than ever I believe that God can indeed do the impossible and there is no person alive in whom God cannot perform miracles.

But now my idealism is at last becoming temperate. Each time I stayed for any amount of time in that tropical climate I was totally defeated by the onslaught of mosquitos and my allergy to them. Coming from Southern California, where heat is eliminated by air-conditioned cars, homes and stores, I now found myself in a much hotter climate grasping gratefully for purified ice cubes. I looked around and saw hunger that was not satisfied, animals that suffered without a Society for the Prevention of Cruelty to Animals, death unsoftened by funeral homes, and lives which could not be dramatically altered.

In the United States we have easy answers for many problems. The government subsidizes our poverty and takes care of us, to a degree, in old age. We have instant food, microwave ovens, immediate news coverage from all points in the world, sophisticated medical treatment and, in general, many comforts that most of mankind has never even dreamed of. Yet even for us, and at times especially for us, the basic problems of mankind like loneliness, physical pain, depression and anxiety can still not be eradicated. To believe otherwise is to be disillusioned.

Many times we mistakenly believe that greatness implies the eradication of problems. In the lives of the people in this book, we have clear examples that such is not the case. For them, like us, pain as well as pleasure ebbed and flowed throughout their lives.

So-called victorious Christian living is not found in the eradication of problems. It is to be found in handling problems with all the resources we can gather of physical well being, emotional growth, and the all-sufficiency of God.

It is a profound relief to know that we are in good company with such an illustrious group of people who in spite of their problems and hurt in this life learned to cope with life and became truly great, both in the eyes of man and of God.

In a different translation from that quoted at the outset of this book, Hebrews 12:1 reads: "Since we have such a huge crowd of men of faith watching us from the grandstands, let us strip off anything that slows us down or holds us back,...and let us run with patience the particular race that God has set before us" (TLB). As was pointed out earlier, Amy Carmichael wrote that she believed that this "huge crowd of men of faith" are literal witnesses, that from heaven they literally observe us, support us, encourage us. Much theological debate has centered around this verse; but I, for one, agree with Miss Carmichael. And my "particular race" that God has set before me has been focused and motivated by the thought that I have the support of such people; their encouragement would not be so great, however, if they had in their lifetimes eradicated all pain and problems. They would not have seemed real. But because they were great yet mortal, I garner inspiration and hope from their lives.

Tonight I walked down by the ocean and watched the tide as it moved relentlessly in and out over the smooth shoreline. The softness of the rocky beach was evidence of the fact that the tide always does go back and forth. It never stays and it never fails to return. So it is with our feelings. Painful and joyful, they do not stay. They leave, they return. And part of the gracefulness of maturity is to know this fact. For no matter how painful things become, the feelings do not remain nor can they be eradicated. For pain in one form or another returns. But again, only for a time. What does remain forever is the One who is God and the host of heavenly beings who surround us with love and care.

His Presence does not guarantee the eradication of need, whether the need be emotional, spiritual or material. But He does guarantee that needs will be met.

As Hudson Taylor began the impossible task of evangelizing inland China, he was told: "You will be forgotten...With no committee or organization before the public, you will be lost sight of in that distant land. Claims are many nowadays. Before long you may find yourselves without even the necessaries of life!"

"I am taking my children with me," was the quiet answer, "and I notice it is not difficult to remember that they need breakfast in the morning, dinner at midday, and supper at night. Indeed, I could not forget them if I tried. And I find it impossible to think that our heavenly Father is less tender and mindful of his children than I, a poor earthly father, am of mine. No, he will not forget us!"[1]

Hudson Taylor's God is our God. He alone, along with Heaven's forces, remains the ultimate source of all our going on.

NOTES

Chapter 2
Divine Spending Money
[1]F.B. Meyer, *Our Daily Homily*, vol. IV, *Isaiah-Malachi* (New York: Fleming H. Revell Company, 1899), 169.
[2]W.Y. Fullerton, D.D., *F.B. Meyer, A Biography*, (London: Marshall, Morgan and Scott Ltd., n.d.), 8.
[3]F.B. Meyer, B.A., D.D., *Peace, Perfect Peace: A Portion for the Sorrowing* (Westwood, N.J.: Fleming H. Revell Company, MDCCCXCVII), 28.
[4]F.B. Meyer, Ibid., 38-40.
[5]Gloria Steinem, *Revolution from Within* (Boston: Little, Brown and Company, 1992), 153.
[6]C.S. Lewis, *Mere Christianity* (New York: Macmillan Publishing Company, Inc., 1964), 160.
[7]F.B. Meyer, *Exodus*, vol. I, Chapters 1-20 (London: The Religious Tract Society, n.d.), 223.
[8]F.B. Meyer, Ibid., 147.
[9]F.B. Meyer, *Christian Living* (New York: Fleming H. Revell Company, 1892), 80-81.
[10]George Matheson, "Make me a captive, Lord," hymn, *Keswick Hymn-Book* (London: Marshall, Morgan and Scott, Ltd., n.d.), 38-39.
[11]Rev. F.B. Meyer, B.A., *Steps into the Blessed Life* (Philadelphia: Henry Atemus Co., 1896), 127.
[12]F.B. Meyer, Ibid., 47.
[13]F.B. Meyer, *Light on Life's Duties*, (Chicago: Bible Institute Colportage Association, 1895), 123.
[14]Rev. C.H. Spurgeon, *Sermons*, vol. II (New York: Funk and Wagnalls Company, n.d.), 147.
[15]Rev. C.H. Spurgeon, *Sermons*, vol. XI, Sermons Preached At The Metropolitan Tabernacle (New York: Funk and Wagnalls Company, n.d.), 81.
[16]G.K. Chesterton, *The End of the Armistice* (London: Sheed and Word, 1940), 18.
[17]Amy Carmichael, *Candles in the Dark: Letters of Amy Carmichael* (Fort Washington, Pa.: Christian Literature Crusade, 1982), 9.
[18]Amy Carmichael, Ibid., 59.

Chapter 3
Wounded Heroes
[1]Francis Thompson, *Hound of Heaven,* poem.
[2]John Donne, *"Batter my heart, three-personed God,"* sonnet.
[3]Henry and Mary Guinness—interview on Geraldine Guinness Taylor of CIM, 6-9-92.
[4]Ibid.
[5]Ruth Bell Graham, interview.
[6]Amy Carmichael, *Gold Cord*, (Fort Washington, PA: Christian Literature Crusade) p. 28.

Chapter 4
F.B. Meyer: Putting Faith into Shoeleather
[1]W.Y. Fullerton, D.D., *F.B. Meyer, A Biography*, (London: Marshall, Morgan and Scott Ltd., n.d.), 59–60.
[2]Ibid., 61.
[3]Ibid.
[4]Ibid., 9.
[5]Ibid.

6Ibid.

7F.B. Meyer, *Light on Life's Duties*, (Chicago: Bible Institute Colportage Association, 1895), 41–42.

8F.B. Meyer, *The Christ-Life for the Self-Life* (Formerly "A Castaway"), (Chicago: Moody Press, n.d.), 126.

9Ibid., 58–59.

10F.B. Meyer, B.A., *The Future Tenses of the Blessed Life* (Chicago: Fleming H. Revell Company, (n.d.), 120–21.

11Ibid., 116–17.

12Rev. F.B. Meyer, B.A., *David: Shepherd, Psalmist, King* (Chicago: Fleming H. Revell Company, 1895), 52.

13F.B. Meyer, *The Present Tenses of the Blessed Life* (London: Marshall, Morgan, and Scott, 1953), 11.

14W.Y. Fullerton, *F.B. Meyer*, 33.

15Ibid.

16Ibid., 37.

17Ibid., 182–83.

18Ibid.

19Rev. F.B. Meyer, B.A., *Steps into the Blessed Life,* (Philadelphia, Henry Altemus Co., 1896) p. 78.

20Ibid., 74–75.

21Ibid., 76–78.

22Ibid., 114–15.

23Ibid., 106–7.

24Ibid., 306.

25Ibid., 82.

26Ibid., 69.

27Ibid., 60.

28Ibid., 272–73.

29F.B. Meyer, *The Prophet of Hope, Studies in Zechariah* (Grand Rapids: Zondervan Publishing House, 1952), 126–27.

30W.Y. Fullerton, *F.B. Meyer*, 184.

31F.B. Meyer, *The Christ-Life for the Self-Life*, 125.

32F.B. Meyer, *Steps into the Blessed Life*, 165.

33F.B. Meyer, B.A., D.D., *Peace, Perfect Peace: A Portion for the Sorrowing* (Westwood, N.J.: Fleming H. Revell Company, MDCCCXCVII), 80.

34F.B. Meyer, *David: Shepherd, Psalmist, King*, 182–83.

35Ibid., 183–85.

36Rev. F.B. Meyer, B.A., *Our Daily Homily*, vol. 5 (Chicago: Fleming H. Revell Company, 1899), 229.

37F.B. Meyer, *Our Daily Homily*, vol. 4, 249.

38F.B. Meyer, B.A., D.D., *Peace, Perfect Peace*, 52–53.

39Ibid., 54–56.

40W.Y. Fullerton, *F.B. Meyer*, 129.

41Ibid., 213.

42Ibid., 215.

43Ibid., 148.

Chapter 5
Amy Carmichael: Triumph in Suffering
[1]Amy Carmichael, *Gold Cord* (Fort Washington, PA: Christian Literature Crusade) p. 3.
[2]Frank Houghton, *Amy Carmichael of Dohnavur* (Fort Washington, PA: Christian Literature Crusade, n.d.), p. 195.
[3]Amy Carmichael, *Toward Jerusalem* (Fort Washington, PA: Christian Literature Crusade, 1961), p. 94.
[4]Amy Carmichael, *Kohila* (Fort Washington, PA: Christian Literature Crusade, n.d.), p. 129.
[5]Ibid., pp. 129, 130.
[6]Ibid., pp. 131, 132.
[7]Amy Carmichael, *Gold by Moonlight* (Fort Washington, PA: Christian Literature Crusade, 1960), p. 48.
[8]Ibid., p. 46.
[9]Carmichael, *Kohila,* p. 97.
[10]Amy Carmichael, *Rose from Brier* (Fort Washington, PA: Christian Literature Crusade, 1972), pp. 18, 19.
[11]Amy Carmichael, *Candles in the Dark* (Fort Washington, PA: Christian Literature Crusade, © 1981), p. 54.
[12]Carmichael, *Gold by Moonlight,* pp. 74, 75.
[13]Amy Carmichael, *Gold Cord* (Fort Washington, PA: Christian Literature Crusade, 1957), p. 268.
[14]Carmichael, *Kohila,* p. 139.
[15]Ibid., p. 134.
[16]Ibid., p. 135.
[17]Ibid., p. 136.
[18]Carmichael, *Gold Cord,* pp. 169, 170.
[19]Carmichael, *Gold by Moonlight,* p. 93.
[20]Ibid., pp. 101, 102.
[21]Amy Carmichael, *Ponnammal* (Fort Washington, PA: Christian Literature Crusade, 1950), pp. 108, 109.
[22]Carmichael, *Rose from Brier,* pp. 112, 113.
[23]Houghton, *Amy Carmichael,* p. 189.
[24]Ibid., p. 373.
[25]Carmichael, *Gold by Moonlight,* p. 36.
[26]Ibid., p. 38.
[27]Carmichael, *Gold Cord,* pp. 69, 70.
[28]Carmichael, *Rose from Brier,* p. XII.

Chapter 6
Charles Spurgeon: Living with Depression
[1]Amy Carmichael, *Gold Cord,* (Fort Washington, PA: Christian Literature Crusade, Inc., 1957), p. 268.
[2]Helmut Thielicke, John W. Doberstein, trans., *Encounter with Spurgeon* (Grand Rapids: Baker Book House, 1975), p. 214. © 1963 by Fortress Press.
[3]Richard E. Day, *The Shadow of the Broad Brim* (Valley Forge: used by permission of Judson Press,

1934), p. 175.
[4]Ibid., p. 85.
[5]Ibid., p. 96.
[6]Ibid., p. 185.
[7]Ibid., p. 197.
[8]Ibid., p. 198.
[9]Ibid., p. 173.
[10]Ibid., p. 173.
[11]Ibid., pp. 177, 178.
[12]Thielicke, op. cit., pp. 218–222.
[13]Ibid., pp. 222, 223.
[14]Charles H. Spurgeon, *Treasury of David* (Grand Rapids: "Taken from *Treasury of David,* by C.H. Spurgeon, edited by David Otis Fuller. © 1940, 1968 by David Otis Fuller. Used by permission of Zondervan Publishing House") vol. 1, p. 110.
[15]Ibid., vol. 3., p. 108.
[16]Charles H. Spurgeon, *New Park Street Pulpit 1858* (London: Banner of Truth Trust, 1964), vol. 4, pp. 400–461.
[17]Thielicke, op. cit., p. 216.
[18]Ernest W. Bacon, *Spurgeon: Heir of the Puritans* (Grand Rapids: William B. Eerdmans Publishing Co., 1968), p. 78.
[19]Thielicke, op. cit., pp. 217, 218.
[20]Ibid., p. 11.
[21]Ibid., p. 215.
[22]Spurgeon, *Treasury,* vol. 2., pp. 3, 4.
[23]Day, op. cit., p. 178.
[24]Ibid., p. 179.
[25]Spurgeon, op. cit., vol. 2, p. 463.
[26]Ibid., pp. 254, 257.
[27]Spurgeon, *New Park Street,* p. 460.
[28]Spurgeon, op. cit., pp. 251, 254.
[29]Day, op. cit., p. 226.
[30]Ibid., p. 113–114.
[31]Ibid., p. 115.
[32]Ibid., p. 227.
[33]Bacon, op. cit., p. 167.

Chapter 7
Hudson Taylor: Drawing on God's Provision
[1]Dr. and Mrs. Howard Taylor, *Hudson Taylor's Spiritual Secret* (Chicago: Moody Press. "Used by permission" China Inland Mission, Robesonia, PA.) p. 120.
[2]Ibid., p. 33, 34, 35, 36.
[3]Ibid., p. 37.
[4]Ibid., p. 43.
[5]Colin M. Turnbull, *The Mountain People* (New York: Simon and Schuster, 1972), p. 292.
[6]George Muller, *The Life of Trust* (New York: Thomas Y. Crowell Company, Pub., 1898), pp. 481–487.

[7]Dr. and Mrs. Howard Taylor, *Hudson Taylor in Early Years, The Growth of a Soul* (London: The China Inland Mission, 1921), pp. 399, 400. As of 1987, republished as *Biography of J. Hudson Taylor,* OMF Books, Littleton, CO. © 1965.

[8]Dr. and Mrs. Howard Taylor, *Hudson Taylor and the China Inland Mission: The Growth of a Work of God* (Newington Green, London: Lutterworth Press, 1958), 476.

[9]Ibid., p. 32.

[10]Ibid., p. 314.

[11]Ibid., p. 315.

[12]Ibid., p. 316.

[13]Taylor, *Spiritual Secret,* pp. 195, 196.

[14]Ibid., pp. 196, 197.

[15]Dr. and Mrs. Howard Taylor, *Hudson Taylor and the China Inland Mission, The Growth of a Work of God* (London: China Inland Mission, 1958), p. 176. As of 1987, republished as *Biography of J. Hudson Taylor,* OMF Books, Littleton, CO. © 1965.

[16]Ibid., p. 204.

[17]Ibid., pp. 290, 291.

[18]Ibid., p. 291.

[19]A.J. Broomhall, *Hudson Taylor and China's Open Century: Book Seven, It Is Not Death To Die* (London: Hodder and Stoughton, Ltd., 1989), 516–17.

Chapter 8
Geraldine Taylor: Divine Renewal

[1]Joy Guinness, *Mrs. Howard Taylor: Her Web of Time* (London: China Inland Mission, n.d.), 93.

[2]Ibid., 94.

[3]Walter A. Elwell, ed., *Evangelical Dictionary of Theology* (Grand Rapids, Mich.: Baker Book House, 1984), 934.

[4]Joy Guinness, *Mrs. Howard Taylor: Her Web of Time,* 36.

[5]Ibid., 201.

[6]Ibid., 124.

[7]Amy Carmichael, *Toward Jerusalem* (Fort Washington, Pa.: Christian Literature Crusade, 1961), 95.

[8]Joy Guinness, *Mrs. Howard Taylor: Her Web of Time,* 322.

[9]Gigi Graham Tchividjian, *Weather of the Heart* (Portland, Or.: Multnomah Press, 1991), 42-43.

[10]Joy Guinness, *Mrs. Howard Taylor: Her Web of Time,* 279.

[11]Dr. and Mrs. Howard Taylor, *Hudson Taylor and the China Inland Mission: The Growth of a Work of God* (London: China Inland Mission, 1958), 528.

[12]Joy Guinness, *Mrs. Howard Taylor: Her Web of Time,* 199.

[13]Ibid., 198.

[14]Geraldine Taylor, foreword to H. Grattan Guinness, A Father's Letter (London: China Inland Mission, n.d.), 6.

[15]Ibid., 6-7.

[16]H. Grattan Guinness, *A Father's Letter,* 9.

[17]Ibid., 10-11.

[18]Ibid., 12-13.

[19]Ibid., 16-18.

20Joy Guinness, *Mrs. Howard Taylor: Her Web of Time*, 198-99.

21Phyllis Thompson, *D.E. Hoste: A Prince with God* (London: China Inland Mission, n.d.), 48.

22Ibid., 101.

23Ibid., 130-31.

24Ibid., 80.

25Ibid., 81.

26Ibid., 116.

27Mrs. Howard Taylor, *Behind the Ranges: Fraser of Lisuland, Southwest China* (London: China Inland Mission, 1956), 84.

28Ibid., 87.

29Ibid., 89.

30Ibid., 89-90.

31Ibid., 91.

32Ibid., 134.

33Ibid., 135.

34Mrs. Howard Taylor, *Pastor HSI: Confucian Scholar and Christian* (London: China Inland Mission, 1949), 49.

35Ibid., 240.

36Ibid., 242.

37Ibid., 291.

38Dr. and Mrs. Howard Taylor, *Hudson Taylor and the China Inland Mission: The Growth of a Work of God*, 509-10.

39Ibid.

40Ibid., 511.

41Ibid., 515.

Chapter 9
Isobel Kuhn: A Platform of Testing

1Isobel Kuhn, *In the Arena* (Chicago: Moody Press, 1958), 33.

2Ibid., 142.

3Ibid., 150.

4Ibid.

5Ibid., 221.

6Ibid.

7Ibid., 212.

8Ibid., 213.

9Ibid., 220.

10Ibid.

11Ibid., 9.

12Ibid., 8.

13Ibid., 35.

14Isobel Kuhn, *Green Leaf in Drought-Time* (Chicago: Moody Press, 1957), 7.

15Carolyn L. Canfield, *One Vision Only* (Chicago: Moody Press, 1959), 60.

16Ibid., 61.

[17]Ibid., 61-62.

[18]Isobel Kuhn, *Precious Things of the Lasting Hills* (Chicago: Moody Press, 1963), 42-43.

[19]Isobel Kuhn, *Nests Above the Abyss* (Philadelphia: China Inland Mission, 1947), 183-84.

[20]Isobel Kuhn, *Precious Things*, 42.

[21]Ibid., 41.

[22]Ibid., 42.

[23]Ibid., 43-44.

[24]Isobel Kuhn, *Stones of Fire* (Chicago: Moody Press, 1960), 9.

[25]Ellice Hopkins, quoted in Ibid., 147.

[26]Isobel Kuhn, *Ascent to the Tribes: Pioneering in North Thailand* (Chicago: Moody Press, 1956), 164.

[27]Dr. F.B. Meyer, as quoted by Isobel Kuhn, *In the Arena* (Chicago: Moody Press, 1958), 184.

[28]Isobel Kuhn, *In the Arena*, 194.

[29]Ibid., 215.

[30]Isobel Kuhn, *Green Leaf in Drought-Time*, 45.

[31]Isobel Kuhn, *In the Arena*, 216.

[32]Amy Carmichael, as quoted by Isobel Kuhn, Ibid., 216.

[33]Isobel Kuhn, Ibid., 216.

[34]Oswald Chambers, as quoted by Isobel Kuhn, *Green Leaf in Drought-Time*, 111.

[35]Isobel Kuhn, *By Searching* (Robesonia, Pa.: OMF Books, 1959), 63-64.

[36]Isobel Kuhn, *In the Arena*, 65.

[37]Isobel Kuhn, *Precious Things*, 33.

[38]Isobel Kuhn, *By Searching*, 67-68.

[39]Ibid.

[40]Isobel Kuhn, *Nests Above the Abyss*, 206.

[41]Isobel Kuhn, *Green Leaf in Drought-Time*, 29-30.

[42]John Stott, *Life in Christ* (Wheaton, Il.: Tyndale House Publishers, Inc., 1991), 83-84.

[43]Isobel Kuhn, *Green Leaf in Drought-Time*, 57-58.

[44]Ibid., 93

[45]Ibid., 94.

[46]Samuel Rutherford, as quoted by Carolyn L. Canfield, *One Vision Only*, 186.

[47]Amy Carmichael, *Candles in the Dark: Letters of Amy Carmichael* (Fort Washington, Pa.: Christian Literature Crusade, 1982), 59.

Chapter 10
C.S. Lewis: Dealing with Imperfection

All material quoted is used by permission.

[1]C.S. Lewis, *The Problem of Pain* (New York: The Macmillan Company, © 1943, 1945, 1952. "Used by permission" William Collins Sons & Co., Ltd., London), p. 9.

[2]Ibid., p. 18.

[3]Ibid., p. 105.

[4]C.S. Lewis, *Mere Christianity* (New York: Macmillan Publishing Company, Inc., 1964. "Used by permission" William Collins Sons & Co., Ltd., London), p. 109.

[5]C.S. Lewis, *A Grief Observed* (New York: The Seabury Press, 1963), © 1961 by N.W. Clerk. Reprinted by permission Harper & Row Publishers, Inc., p. 36.

6Ibid., p. 43.

7Ibid., pp. 8, 9.

8Lewis, *Mere Christianity,* pp. 180–182.

9C.S. Lewis, *Surprised by Joy* (Orlando, Florida: Harcourt Brace Jovanovich, Inc., 1956), p. 21.

10C.S. Lewis, *Reflections on the Psalms* (Orlando, Florida: Harcourt Brace Jovanovich, Inc., 1964), p. 28.

11C.S. Lewis, *The Weight of Glory* (Grand Rapids: William B. Eerdmans Publishing Company, 1965), © by the executors of the Estate of C.S. Lewis, 1967. "Used by permission" William Collins Sons & Co., Ltd., London, pp. 40, 41.

12Ibid., pp. 14, 15.

13C.S. Lewis, *Christian Reflections* (Grand Rapids: William B. Eerdmans Publishing Company, 1974) "Used by permission" William Collins Sons & Co., Ltd., London, p. 39.

14Ibid., p. 42.

15Ibid., p. 43.

16Ibid.

17W.H. Lewis, ed., *Letters of C.S. Lewis* (Orlando, Florida: Reprinted by permission Harcourt Brace Jovanovich, Inc., 1975), pp. 118–120. © 1966 by W.H. Lewis and executors of C.S. Lewis.

18Lewis, *Weight of Glory,* p. 52.

19C.S. Lewis, *Letters to an American Lady* (Grand Rapids: William B. Eerdmans Publishing Company, 1967), p. 73.

20C.S. Lewis, *Mere Christianity,* pp. 84–86.

21Ibid., p. 116.

22Ibid., pp. 88, 89.

23Ibid., p. 92.

24Ibid., p. 172.

25Ibid., p. 174.

26Ibid., pp. 174, 175.

Chapter 11
Ruth Bell Graham: Reference Points

1Ruth Bell Graham, *It's My Turn* (Old Tappan, N.J.: Power Books, Fleming H. Revell Company, 1973), 173.

2Ibid.

3John Pollock, *A Foreign Devil in China,* The Story Of Dr. L. Nelson Bell (Minneapolis, Minn.: World Wide Publications, 1971), 113.

4Ibid., 203.

5Ibid., 113.

6Ruth Bell Graham, *Prodigals and Those Who Love Them,* (Colorado Springs, Co.: Focus on the Family, 1991), 76.

7Patricia Daniels Cornwell, *A Time for Remembering,* The Story of Ruth Bell Graham (New York: Harper and Row Publishers, 1983), 18.

8Ibid., 71.

9Ruth Bell Graham, poem, quoted in Ibid., 39.

10Ruth Bell Graham, *It's My Turn,* 72.

11C.S. Lewis, *The Silver Chair* (New York: Collier Books, Division of Macmillan Publishing Co.,

Inc., 1976), 207.
[12]Ruth Bell Graham, *It's My Turn*, 62-63.
[13]Frank W. Boreham, D.D., *Mountains in the Mist* (London: The Epworth Press, 1933), 174.
[14]Ruth Bell Graham, as quoted in Patricia Daniels Cornwell, *A Time for Remembering*, 179-80.
[15]Ibid., p. 158.
[16]Ibid., p. 160.
[17]Ibid., p, 172.
[18]Ibid., p. 121.
[19]F.W. Boreham, *Mountains in the Mist*, p. 130.
[20]Ruth Bell Graham, *A Time for Remembering*, p. 140.

Chapter 12
Living Within an Eternal Perspective
[1]Dr. and Mrs. Howard Taylor, *Hudson Taylor's Spiritual Secret* (Chicago: Moody Press, Used by Permission, Littleton, CO., OMF) 124.

Footnotes for Vignettes
No Scar?
[1]Amy Carmichael, *Toward Jerusalem* (Fort Washington, PA.: Christian Literature Crusade, 1961), 85.

D. Martyn Lloyd-Jones
[1]D. Martyn Lloyd-Jones, *Authority* (London: Inter-Varsity Fellowship, 1958), 29.
[2]Ibid., 21.

Andrew Murray
[1]V. Raymond Edman, *They Found the Secret* (Grand Rapids, Mich.: Zondervan Publishing Company, 1965), 97–98.

Frances Ridley Havergal
[1]Frances Ridley Havergal, poem, as quoted in Joy Guinness, *Mrs. Howard Taylor: Her Web of Time* (London: China Inland Mission, 1952), 368.
[2]Frances Ridley Havergal, *My King* (London: James Nisbet and Company, Ltd., 1878), 30–32.

Handley C.G. Moule
[1]H.C.G. Moule, *Thoughts on Union with Christ,* as quoted by Amy Carmichael, *If* (Fort Washington, PA.: Christian Literature Crusade, 1960), 34.
[2]Amy Carmichael, *Gold by Moonlight* (Fort Washington, PA.: Christian Literature Crusade, 1960), 34.

Dwight L. Moody
[1]S. Spurgeon, as quoted by A.P. Fitt, *The Life of D.L. Moody* (Moody Press, n.d.), 45.
[2]A.P. Fitt, *The Life of D.L. Moody,* 5.

Brother Lawrence
[1]Brother Lawrence, *The Practice of the Presence of God (Being Conversations and Letters of Nicholas Herman of Lorraine)* (Westwood, N.J., Fleming H. Revell Company, MCMLVII), 6–7.

H.A. Ironside
[1]H.A. Ironside, Litt. D., *Addresses on the First Epistle to the Corinthians* (Neptune, NJ.: Loizeaux Brothers, Inc.), 353–354.

Arthur T. Pierson
[1]Dr. Arthur T. Pierson, *The Bible and Spiritual Life* (London: James Nisbet and Co., Ltd., 1908), 376–77.
[2]Dr. Arthur T. Pierson, "Christ Our Wisdom From God", *The Ministry of Keswick,* edited by Herbert F. Stevenson (Grand Rapids, MI.: Zondervan Publishing House, 1963), 114.

George MacDonald
[1]Rolland Hein, *The World of George MacDonald* (Wheaton, IL.: Harold Shaw Publishers, 1978), 60.
[2]Ibid., 148–49.
[3]Ibid., 77.
[4]George MacDonald, *Diary of an Old Soul* (Minneapolis, MN.: Augsburg Publishing House, 1975), 25.

G. Campbell Morgan
[1]G. Campbell Morgan, *Hosea: The Heart and Holiness of God* (Westwood, N.J.: Fleming H. Revell Company, MCMXXXIV), 105–6.
[2]G. Campbell Morgan, D.D., *The Life of the Christian* (London: Pickering & Inglis Ltd., n.d.), 11.
[3]Ibid., 65–66.
[4]Ibid., 54.

Rotherham, Ironside, Graham, Moule
[1]Joseph Bryant Rotherham, *Rotherham Emphasized Bible, New Testament* (Grand Rapids, MI.: Kregel Publications, 1992), 232.
[2]H.A. Ironside, Litt. D., *Hebrews, James Peter* (Neptune, NJ: Loizeaux Brothers, 1932), 150–51.
[3]Ruth Bell Graham, "If Only", poem.
[4]Handley C.G. Moule, D.D., *Messages from the Epistle to the Hebrews* (London: Elliot Stock, 1909), 81–83.